TABLE OF CONTENTS

COMPLETE SPANISH WORKBOOK FOR ADULT BEGINNERS

Essentials Spanish Words and
Phrases You Need to Know

Explore to Win

Ready To Start Speaking Spanish?

Inside this Complete Spanish Phrasebook
+ digital Spanish flashcards combo you'll:

✓ **Say what you want:** learn the most common words and phrases used in Spanish, so you can express yourself clearly, the first time!

✓ **Avoid awkward fumbling:** explore core Spanish grammar principles to avoid situations where you're left blank, not knowing what to say.

✓ **Improved recall:** Confidently express yourself in Spanish by learning high-frequency verbs & conjugations - taught through fun flashcards!

INTRODUCTION

Imagine you're on a vacation with your family in a native Spanish-speaking country. You're all enjoying a beautiful beach when a waiter approaches you to take your order. His English isn't the best, so there's bound to be issues ordering the food and beverages without mistakes. Are you able to take control of the conversation in Spanish to communicate exactly what you want? Can you provide the meal your family desires without problems or miscommunication?

Spanish is easily one of the most important languages in the modern era. With more than 500 million Spanish speakers around the world, it's no wonder that so many people are interested and willing to learn this beautiful language. It's relevant for business conversations, traveling, and often even small talk in your hometown. There are plenty of cultural products in Spanish such as books, movies, and music that can only be truly enjoyed with a good understanding of the Spanish language. This means that there's a good portion of the world that you're missing just by being unable to have a conversation in Spanish, which is what brought you to this book in the first place. You need a fast and reliable way to learn Spanish, and this book has been designed for you.

By going through the following chapters, you'll learn everything that you need to have casual conversations, be productive in a professional environment, understand written Spanish texts, and handle yourself while visiting a Spanish-speaking country. The knowledge in these pages has been structured and reinforced with examples and exercises in order to make sure it's cemented in your brain. You'll know how to speak Spanish for the rest of your life; and if you happen to forget minor details, its simple design will help you navigate the book with ease and revise whatever knowledge you need to refresh.

Without a doubt, learning a new language is one of the best things we can do, since it will not only help us to expand our knowledge more and more, but it will also be very helpful for any occasion that we have it. Similarly, in terms of work, learning such a popular language is one of the best things we can do for our career, as it will help us further expand our resume, and thus be able to have many new job opportunities. It is confirmed that bilingual people have many more opportunities in today's world of work, especially considering that we live in a world that has gone through a process of globalization, which means that the vast majority of companies need proactive people who are able to communicate in other languages. Many people believe that learning a language is only for when we go on vacation or something, but the truth is that this has countless short-term and long-term benefits for us, apart from the fact that learning a language is also a lot of fun.

Every day that you spend without learning Spanish is a day further away from your goal. Tomorrow you could find yourself in a situation where a couple of Spanish phrases will be the difference between making a good or a bad impression. This book promises to prepare you for these sorts of situations. All you need to do is go through the chapters in order, pay attention, and do the activities. You already know why you should do it, and you have the way to do it in front of you, all that's left for you now is to take the first step with the following chapter.

CHAPTER 1:

LEARNING A NEW LANGUAGE

Most people around the world are constantly looking for a way to be a more complete person, and of course, more intelligent. Learning a new language is one of the easiest and most wonderful ways we have to strengthen our personal growth, as well as to add much more knowledge to our minds. However, when we take care of learning to speak a language as popular and wonderful as Spanish, this becomes even more interesting, since it is not only a language that will serve us for the two things that we mentioned above but also will serve us in many other aspects of our lives since this is one of the most widely spoken languages in the world. Of course, we all know that English is the universal language, and therefore the most important of all.

However, there are more than 460 million native speakers of Spanish in the world, which tells us about the enormous importance of learning a language as popular as this one. In fact, Spanish is the most learned language throughout the universities in the United States, since numerous statistics show that more than 50% of American students choose to learn to speak Spanish every year, a figure that is undoubtedly enormous. There are many people who believe that Spanish is only spoken in South American countries, but the truth is that it is spoken in many other countries around the world.

Of course, South America is the continent where Spanish is spoken the most since all of its countries (with the exception of Brazil and Guyana) have Spanish as their official language. In addition, in some other countries such as Mexico, the Dominican Republic, Puerto Rico, Cuba, and Spain, Spanish is also spoken as the official language. Each of these countries has a different way of adapting Spanish since even in many of those countries, such as Spain, there are other unofficial alternative languages that are spoken in certain provinces. The point is that Spanish is a language spoken in many countries, so learning this wonderful language will bring us numerous advantages, regardless of the main reason why we are learning it.

For example, there are many people who want to speak Spanish for work reasons, since this would allow them to expand their resume and access many more opportunities in the business world, especially if we take into account that today we live in a world so globalized and dynamic where all business is done globally. In the same way, there are many other people who only want to learn to speak Spanish as a form of self-improvement, since they know that in this way they will expand their knowledge even more, just as they will be able to exercise their brain in various cognitive areas. like memory, multitasking, and many other things. The point is that no matter the reason why we are learning Spanish since this is going to be very useful to us in many aspects of our lives, therefore, the main objective of this book is that we can learn everything necessary to develop an excellent level of Spanish, on par with that of a native speaker.

The pace of learning of people is not the same, it depends on the capabilities of each one, our dedication, and our motivations. Learning Spanish, like any other language, can be simple and fun if we adapt the method to the way each of us learns. To speak a language well it is necessary to invest a certain amount of time. Once the base is acquired and the fear of ridicule is overcome, everything will go much faster. Set yourself small challenges, reward yourself for achievements, and above all, enjoy your progress. This means that we cannot pretend to learn to speak a language perfectly in a matter of a few days, since it requires a lot of effort, motivation, and dedication.

A Little Bit of History

Like most of the languages we know today, Spanish is a language that was born from Common Latin (also known as Vulgar Latin). This language was born thousands of years ago in the Iberian Peninsula, which today is a region that is part of Spain and Portugal. However, it was not until the year 1200 that this language began to become popular in Spain and, basically, little by little it became the official language of that country, which was the first to make it its official language.

In fact, different versions of the language began to be formed in that country, since not only was Castilian spoken (which is the most common way of speaking Spanish) but Andalusian and Catalan were also formed.

Hundreds of years later, at the time of colonization, Spain was the country that was in charge of discovering and conquering most of the countries of America. That is why from the year 1600, this language began to be quite popular in countries such as Venezuela, Colombia, Ecuador, Argentina, Bolivia, Peru, Chile, Uruguay, and many other countries on the continent. Little by little this language was mixed among the natives until it became the official language a few years after each of those countries.

However, despite being the country where this language originated and being the country that made it popular throughout the world, today Spain has less than 10% of all Spanish-speaking people, which undoubtedly speaks of the extensive growth and expansion that this language has had throughout the world.

Tips to Learn a New Language

There are many methods and ways that will help us speed up this entire learning process and make it much more comfortable. In this way, we will be able to feel much more satisfied throughout this process, so that in this way we make sure to learn each of these topics perfectly. One of those methods that we can use is to read books or articles in Spanish. When we read, we not only expand our knowledge, but we will also become aware of many grammatical structures and new words that will help us carry out this learning process in the best possible way. That is why it is always recommended to read in Spanish so that we can learn to pronounce each of the words that we see, just as we learn each of the grammatical structures that we are going to see throughout this book.

Another way in which we can accelerate this learning process is by listening to music in Spanish. This is not only a good learning method, but we are also going to be able to have a lot of fun and be able to learn some of the slang and popular words that are said daily in Spanish.

The good thing is that today music in Spanish is quite popular around the world, as well as some podcasts that we can listen to, enjoy and take advantage of to learn some of the most important things about this incredible language. Finally, we can also practice watching movies entirely in Spanish, and putting the subtitles in English. In this way, we are going to make sure that we understand everything that they are saying in the film and that we can understand the way in which people commonly speak to you in Spanish.

However, the method that has been proven throughout history as the most effective when it comes to consolidating ourselves speaking a new language is to practice with another person who also knows how to speak Spanish or is learning. If it is a person who already knows how to speak perfect Spanish, it will be excellent since we are going to have a person who can correct our mistakes when pronouncing or writing something, as well as tell us some of the easiest ways in which we can learn certain grammatical structures. Similarly, when we talk to a person who already knows how to speak Spanish perfectly, we are going to be practicing various factors such as listening and speaking, which are often the most difficult to master.

If we practice with a person who, like us, is just learning the language, then we will also have the advantage that we will not feel sorry if we make a mistake or make a mistake, since we know that this is likely to happen to them as well. to the other person. Through this method, we can also encourage each other to continue learning all the wonders of this language that undoubtedly has a lot to offer us, and that has shown that if we put all our efforts we can achieve incredible things in a very short time. The important thing is that we are not afraid of making mistakes because although none of us is perfect, we can all learn the wonders of this language much easier than we imagine.

Never Stop Learning

When we commit to learning a new language, the process is similar to when we first got married. In other words, we will have to make a commitment that lasts for our entire lives, since a language is not learned in a matter of days, but rather requires a lot of practice and experience over the years. When learning a new language, especially one as complex as Spanish, we must be willing to spend several hours a day practicing and be willing to do everything necessary so that each of the things we learn remains engraved in our memory forever. permanently. Many people learn languages at school, university, or even when they are just children, but over time they forget everything they learned.

This is because the languages must be practiced on a regular basis, and if possible, every day of the week. Practicing a language takes only a few minutes a day, especially if we use any of the methods that we saw in the previous section since they can help us achieve great things and learn much faster. People often believe that to learn a new language it is necessary that we have a lot of free time and that we spend all day practicing and studying when the truth is that just a few minutes a day are enough for us to learn a language permanently. and in a perfect way, as long as we maintain a high level of discipline and perseverance throughout the process since otherwise, everything will be in vain.

It's Not Easy, but It's Not Impossible

Many times people believe that Spanish is very difficult since it has some grammatical structures that are quite complex, and above all that sentences are usually much longer than those formed in English. However, it is important that we know that for many people English is the most difficult language because, despite the fact that it is a language that seems quite simple, it has certain things that can be very complex for the person who is learning. The most important thing is that we must know that learning to speak Spanish perfectly is not something impossible since all the people in this world have the ability to learn to speak a new language in a matter of a few months. The problem is that not all people are willing to invest in their education, as well as in taking the time to study and practice each of the things that we are going to learn in this book.

We must always keep a long-term vision and think about all the benefits that we will obtain once we have completely mastered this language since this will bring us many good things in life. Of course, this process is not easy, since it involves many aspects in which we will have to put our maximum effort and dedication, as well as our maximum potential to learn all these things. That is why I am sure that you will master each of the lessons that we are going to see next, just as you will strive to learn a little every day and thus become a true expert.

Things You Need to Know to Take Advantage of This Book

Throughout this book, we are going to see through the different chapters certain valuable lessons that are going to teach us the most important things that we must learn about Spanish. The good thing is that through these chapters we are not only going to learn the various meanings of some of the most important things in this language, but we are also going to see the exact pronunciations that should be given to each of the words. and phrases that we are learning. That is why, to get the most out of this book, we must make sure to review each of the lessons as many times as necessary, since usually once is not enough to learn perfectly.

In the same way, we must make sure to take note of everything that seems interesting to us, as well as all the things that seem difficult to us, since in this way we can put together a notebook where we put everything that we are learning and So have it on hand in case of any eventuality. Many times what happens to us during reading is that after we read we simply forget about the content, not because we did not want to learn it, but because as we have received so much information there are certain things that can confuse us or remain far behind in our memory. Instead, by taking notes we are going to make sure that each one of those things that we are learning we always have with us, and therefore everything we learn remains in our memory forever.

Another important factor that we must take into account when reading this book is that learning a language is not about translating what we want to say, but about understanding and interpreting everything we are saying, reading, hearing, or writing. so that we can develop this language naturally just as we do with English. All languages are made up of four extremely important factors, which are speaking, writing, listening, and reading. Each of them is extremely important and will help us learn that language perfectly. That is why this book is designed so that we can practice these four factors. Therefore, in addition to reading, we recommend that after each lesson, you write your own examples using the information learned in that lesson.

For example, when we are in the professions lesson, we can write several sentences detailing what we work at and what our parents work at. For the speaking part, it will be very important that after we see the examples, we not only read them but also pronounce them out loud so that we can practice the different forms of pronunciation that each of those phrases and words has. Finally, in the listening part, what we can do is watch a video on YouTube about the lesson we just read in the book, so that we can understand much more and see examples of everyday life in each of the lessons. those lessons.

Best of all is that at the end of the book we will have a short article available that will allow us to read it completely in Spanish. Don't worry, this article will be translated in its entirety so that we can compare each of the grammatical structures that we learned throughout the book and we can perfectly understand its meaning in English. This is one of the most basic but most complete ways we have to learn, so we must take advantage of this article to enhance our level of reading and interpretation in Spanish.

The good thing is that this article will be about something curious about some cities in South America, so that you not only practice Spanish, but you can also learn and have fun with some curiosities of that continent and learn more about its culture. That is why, without a doubt, this book is a complete adventure ideal for all those people who want to learn to speak Spanish once and for all and thus be able to achieve one of their most desired goals.

Also, Remember This is Not a Race

One of the most common mistakes people make when learning a new language, and one of the reasons why so many people end up giving up and abandoning this path, is that they think they will see immediate results. However, we must understand that this whole process is a marathon, and not a 100-meter race like the ones Usain Bolt used to do. This means that one of the keys to learning a new language is to have a lot of patience, otherwise, we will simply never be able to achieve our goals. When we are children, and our parents start talking to us and saying words that they want us to repeat, we do not learn to speak English immediately, but it is also a process of learning, growth, and development that occurs little by little.

That is why we cannot pretend to become experts speaking Spanish in a matter of just a few days since no one has ever achieved something like this. On the other hand, if we have the necessary patience, and above all, we make sure to practice every day, even for half an hour, then without a doubt we will be able to master this wonderful language much faster than we think.

Many times it can be a bit difficult to maintain that level of consistency when we are learning since in our daily routine we also have to study, work, take our children to school, cook, go to the market, and of course, socialize from time to time. when. However, everyone has the same 24 hours a day available, so it is not a valid excuse to say that we do not have time. It all depends on how we distribute our free hours and what we dedicate ourselves to right now. For example, if we only watch Netflix in our free time, then it is very likely that we will not be able to achieve our goals since we will not be dedicating the necessary time to learning.

Of course, each one of us loves to watch a good movie from time to time, but we have to know that there are moments that we have to dedicate to learning Spanish since otherwise we simply will not be able to achieve the objective to master this language perfectly. That is why we must put together a weekly schedule that includes at least half an hour every day, which we are going to dedicate to practicing Spanish. This is the only magic formula that will allow us to learn this language correctly.

The Technique of Shadowing

This is a great method to learn to speak Spanish (or any other language, of course). It is based on a very simple concept: listen and repeat what we have just heard by exactly reproducing the intonations, pauses, etc. That is to say, to act as if we were real parrots. For this, it is important that you know well what you are repeating. If you listen to a song in Spanish, print the lyrics. If you decide to watch a video, look for a subtitled file. He then listened to a phrase, paused, and repeated that process. It may seem like a very simple exercise at first glance, but don't be fooled; it is more complicated than it seems. It is a very effective activity that will allow you to learn by leaps and bounds. This is a method that is often quite underestimated, but that can give us many benefits if we do it consistently.

In the same way, it can be quite effective if you can learn together with a native person from a country where Spanish is spoken. However, if this is not possible, speak to yourself out loud in Spanish and record yourself. Try to think ahead about what words native speakers choose, as well as how they use the language. Also, try to imitate them in pronunciation, intonation, and melody. It may seem a little forced at first, but you think that over time it will help you have a more natural diction. This is a good practice that will only take you 10 minutes a day.

At the same time that you speak in Spanish, you will be recording your day. Plus, you can check your pronunciation later by listening to yourself. Many times, after hearing what we just said, we realize our mistakes so that we can correct them the next time. Also, repetition gives you the opportunity to assess whether you sound the same as a native speaker.

CHAPTER 2:

BASICS

We'll go over the fundamental points and words of the English language. Of course, the idea of this book is for us to learn to speak Spanish the right way, but in order to do that, we first need to understand certain fundamental concepts in English, and then we can go from there to learn Spanish or whatever other languages we want to learn. The problem of many people is that they want to learn a new language without having a perfect command of English, which is a problem because if we do not understand certain things in English, then we will not be able to interpret and learn many of the grammatical rules present in the Spanish language.

The good thing is that the vast majority of these things that we are going to see about the English language are things that we use on a daily basis. However, many times we do not realize certain things or certain technicalities since we do it automatically and we are not aware of that type of thing.

Fundamental Differences

As a native English speaker, you'll need to understand these concepts before you start learning Spanish. Little by little, we will realize that Spanish and English are very different in many things, and it is important that we know each of these differences so that we can have a much simpler and more efficient learning process. Knowing all these differences is one of the keys that we will need to learn to speak and understand Spanish perfectly.

Many people believe that they only have to learn to translate a few words and that way they will know how to speak another language, but the truth is that this learning process is much more complex than this, since we must also know each of the grammatical structures involved, as well as certain rules of the language. That is why the objective of this introductory chapter is for us to become much more familiar with this wonderful language.

Nouns Have Gender

English relies on pronouns to convey the gender of a person, but that's not exactly the case in Spanish. In Spanish, not only do people and animals have a gender, but also every other noun. So if you look at a word such as "máscara" (mask), it's feminine, while "cinturón" (belt) is a masculine noun. It's often the case that words that end with "o" or "e" are masculine, and those that end with "a" are feminine. However, there are far too many exceptions to this rule to take it as the only foundation for this rule.

Instead, practice is the only real way to learn the gender of all nouns. You'll learn the gender of any particular noun by paying attention to the articles, adjectives, and participle verbs used around it. These are the groups of words that change with the gender of the noun, and you'll learn about them further in the book.

Diacritic Acute

This is the name of the famous "tilde" (´) you'll see used often in Spanish. You don't need to concern yourself regarding when to use it and not to use it while you're writing; you'll learn this by reading Spanish texts. What you need to understand is that the job of the tilde is to mark the strong syllable of the word. It's true that all words have a strong syllable in their pronunciation, and not all Spanish words have a tilde.

However, this makes it easier to pronounce the words with a tilde, while the main use of the tilde is to differentiate two words that are written the same way but pronounced differently.

Let's see a couple of example words with their pronunciation to illustrate the use of the tilde:

Word	Pronunciation	Translation
Pájaro	PAH-hah-roh	Bird
Canción	Can-SEEOHN	Song
Árbol	AHR-bohl	Tree
Jardín	Har-DEEN	Garden

Punctuation Marks

Unlike English, Spanish uses two interrogation (question) marks (¿?) and/or two exclamation marks (¡!). Questions and exclamations are marked in Spanish from the beginning by an opening punctuation mark (in this case, "¡" for exclamations and "¿" for questions).

Here are two examples of how this would look like, with their respective pronunciations and translations:

¿Qué te gustaría comer?

Keh teh goos-tah-ree-ah coh-mehr

What would you like to eat?

¡Me alegra que estés aquí!

Meh ah-leh-grah keh ehs-tehs ah-kee

I'm glad you're here!

The Alphabet

Unlike letters in English, letters in Spanish are almost always pronounced the same way, especially the vowels. However, their pronunciation, if stable, is still slightly different from English pronunciation.

De igual manera, poco a poco nos vamos a ir dando cuenta que en el alfabeto del idioma español hay algunas letras que no existen en inglés. Por lo general, esas son las letras que generan una dificultad mayor a la hora de pronunciarlas, ya que es normal debido a que las personas nunca las han oído o visto anteriormente. Lo bueno es que de resto no existen diferencias tan abismales entre un alfabeto y otro, por lo que no se nos hará muy difícil poder aprenderlo.

A: Ah, as in "bar."

B: Beh, as in "ball."

C: Seh. It's pronounced like the C in "race" when it precedes I or E. However, it has a hard pronunciation that resembles more the K pronunciation when it precedes A, U, or O (as in "car").

19

CH: Cheh, as in "cheese." This letter is not always present in the Spanish alphabet.

D: Deh, as in "doll."

E: Eh, as in "get."

F: Eh-feh, as in "fall."

G: Heh, and it has a soft pronunciation and a hard pronunciation. It has a hard pronunciation when it appears before U, O, A, or any consonant, and the pronunciation resembles that of the G in "good." It has a soft pronunciation that resembles the H in "horn" when it goes before E or I. There's an exception to this rule if the G appears before a U and then an E or an I, the U isn't pronounced and the G takes the hard pronunciation; and in that same case, if the U has an umlaut diaeresis (as "güe" or "güi"), the G still has the hard pronunciation, but the U is no longer silent.

H: Ah-cheh, and it's silent, as in "honor."

I: Ee, as in "think."

J: Hoh-tah, pronounced like the H in "hell."

K: Kah, as in "kebab."

L: Eh-leh, as in "loom." When two Ls are placed together, then it's pronounced like the hard Y in words like "yard."

M: Eh-meh, as in "Moon."

N: Eh-neh, as in "nose."

ñ: Ehn-nee-eh. This letter has no equivalent in the English language, and its pronunciation is difficult for native English speakers. Think about common Spanish words that have it such as "jalapeño" and you'll learn its pronunciation.

O: Oh, as in "boat."

P: Peh, as in "pear."

Q: Coo, and it's pronounced like the hard C, like the C in "car." The Q is always followed by a silent U before the main vowel.

R: Eh-reh, as in "race." When it's placed at the beginning of the word, or when two Rs are placed together, then it takes the pronunciation of the hard Spanish R that's made by rolling the Rs, very similar to the pronunciation of "rage," only stronger. When it's a single R in the middle of the word, then the pronunciation is a soft R, as in "art."

S: Eh-seh, as in "soft."

T: Teh, as in "tea."

U: Oo, as the oo in "good." The exception of this rule is when the U is silent (after a Q or a G without a diaeresis umlaut).

V: Veh, as in "vampire."

W: Doh-bleh beh (which means double v). Words with W in Spanish are adaptations of English words, so it also shares the pronunciation with these words, as it happens with "web."

X: Eh-kees, pronounced like the h in "has."

Y: Yeh, pronounced as a hard Y if it precedes a vowel, as in "yearn." However, if it stands alone, it's pronounced like the Spanish I as EE.

Z: Seh-tah, as in "zoo."

Numbers

Without a doubt, numbers are one of the most basic, yet most important things in any language. We can say that in each of the conversations that we carry out in our day to day, we use numbers, either to indicate some amount, some amount of money, or anything else. This means that when we learn a new language, it is mandatory that we learn the different ways in which numbers should be said. Many times people do not give much importance to this since they believe that it is only enough to write a number numerically.

The truth is that it is also very important that we know the correct way in which we should pronounce ourselves so that we can easily identify them when reading or talking to another person. Not knowing the numbers in Spanish is like wanting to learn to play baseball and not knowing what a bat or a ball is, that is, to learn this wonderful language correctly we have to learn everything we need about numbers. As in English, there are cardinal and ordinal numbers, so below we are going to see some of the main differences between them.

It is also important that we know how to differentiate some key factors between the way of pronouncing numbers between one language and the other. For example, when we are going to talk about the fortune that Elon Musk has, we say that he has 100 Billion dollars.

However, in Spanish we should not say that it has "100 billion dollars," but we say that it has "100 billion dollars." This is a rule that often confuses many people, and it is normal that it generates confusion since the translation is a little different from the way it is used in most Spanish-speaking countries. There are very few differences when we talk about numbers in Spanish and numbers in English.

Cardinal Numbers

In this section we are going to focus on cardinal numbers, which are all those that we use on a daily basis to express some quantity, an amount of money, or something similar. In other words, knowing these numbers is going to help us a lot to express ourselves in a better way, especially in certain situations where we must perfectly master this topic. Let's imagine that we are on vacation with our family, and we want to order a meal in a restaurant. In that case, we must know the numbers in order to be able to order the correct quantity, as well as to be able to ask what the various dishes on the menu cost.

In the same way, we are going to need to know the cardinal numbers for the vast majority of things that we are going to say or ask, especially if we are learning Spanish for work reasons. In the same way, as usual, we are going to have a small section dedicated to the pronunciation of each one of those numbers, so that you not only know how they are written but you can also have a practical guide that helps you in the pronunciation of each one. of those numbers.

Number	Spanish Cardinal Name	Pronunciation
0	Cero	Seh-roh
1	Uno	Oo-noh
2	Dos	Dohs
3	Tres	Trehs

4	Cuatro	Cooah-troh
5	Cinco	Seen-coh
6	Seis	Seh-ees
7	Siete	See-eh-teh
8	Ocho	O-choh
9	Nueve	Nooeh-beh
10	Diez	Dee-ehs
11	Once	Ohn-seh
12	Doce	Doh-seh
13	Trece	Treh-she
14	Catorce	Cah-tohr-seh
15	Quince	Keen-seh
16	Dieciséis	Dee-eh-see-seh-ees
17	Diecisiete	Dee-eh-see-eh-teh
18	Dieciocho	Dee-eh-seeoh-choh
19	Diecinueve	Dee-eh-see-nooeh-beh
20	Veinte	Beh-een-teh
21	Veintiuno	Beh-een-teeoo-noh
22	Veintidós	Beh-een-tee-dohs
23	Veintitrés	Beh-een-tee-trehs
24	Veinticuatro	Beh-een-tee-cooah-troh
25	Veinticinco	Beh-een-tee-seen-coh

26	Veintiséis	Beh-een-tee-seh-ees
27	Veintisiete	Beh-een-tee-see-eh-teh
28	Veintiocho	Beh-een-teeoh-choh
29	Veintinueve	Beh-een-tee-nooeh-beh
30	Treinta	Treh-een-tah
31	Treinta y uno	Treh-een-tah ee oo-noh
32	Treinta y dos	Treh-een-tah ee dohs
33	Treinta y tres	Treh-een-tah ee trehs
40	Cuarenta	Cooah-rehn-tah
50	Sincuenta	Seen-cooehn-tah
60	Sesenta	Seh-sehn-tah
70	Setenta	Seh-tehn-tah
80	Ochenta	Oh-chehn-tah
90	Noventa	Noh-behn-tah
100	Cien	See-ehn
101	Ciento uno	See-ehn-toh oo-noh
200	Doscientos	Dohs-see-ehn-tohs
300	Trescientos	Trehs-see-ehn-tohs
400	Cuatrocientos	Cooah-troh-see-ehn-tohs
500	Quinientos	Kee-nee-ehn-tohs
600	Seiscentos	Seh-ees-see-ehn-tohs
700	Setecientos	Seh-teh-see-ehn-tohs

800	Ochocientos	Oh-choh-see-ehn-tohs
900	Novecientos	Noh-beh-see-ehn-tohs
1.000	Mil	Meel
1.500	Mil quinientos	Meel kee-nee-ehn-tohs
2.000	Dos mil	Dohs meel
100.000	Cien mil	See-ehn meel
150.000	Ciento cincuenta mil	See-ehn-toh seen-cooehn-tah meel
1.000.000	Un millón	Oon mee-yohn

Ordinal Numbers

Ordinal numbers are also important but are used to a lesser extent when compared to cardinal numbers. However, if we are learning this language for work purposes, it is very important that we know everything related to ordinal numbers since they are going to be very important when we talk about processes, positions, or anything else similar. We may not use them as much as the cardinal numbers, but it is still very important that we learn to identify and know the correct way to pronounce each of these numbers.

If we like sports, this is one of the most important things we must learn, since they will always be present in any event or competition of this magnitude.

26

Number	Spanish Ordinal Name	Pronunciation
1	Primero	Pree-meh-roh
2	Segundo	Seh-goon-doh
3	Tercero	Tehr-seh-roh
4	Cuarto	Cooahr-toh
5	Quinto	Keen-toh
6	Sexto	Sex-toh
7	Séptimo	Sehp-tee-moh
8	Octavo	Ohc-tah-boh
9	Noveno	Noh-beh-noh
10	Décimo	Deh-see-moh

We'll use a couple of example phrases with numbers to help you remember them. Remember, we'll always look at the pronunciation and translation of each Spanish phrase.

Esta es la segunda vez que veo esta película.

Ehs-tah ehs lah seh-goon-dah behs keh beh-oh ehs-tah peh-lee-coo-lah.

This is the second time I have seen this movie.

Ella tiene cinco perros en su casa.

Eh-yah tee-eh-neh seen-coh peh-rros ehn soo cah-sah

She has five dogs at her home.

Hay veinticuatro alumnos en mi clase.

Ah-ee beh-een-tee-cooah-troh ah-loom-nohs ehn mee clah-seh

There are twenty-five students in my class.

Personal Pronouns

Personal pronouns are another of the most important things when learning a language since all of them allow us to be able to refer to people in a correct way and thus they can understand us perfectly. If we don't know all these personal pronouns, then it will be very difficult for us to start a conversation with someone, since we don't know how to address them in conversation. The good thing is that, just like in English, personal pronouns are quite easy to understand and learn, since the vast majority of them are made up of just a few syllables.

Of course, nowadays the subject of personal pronouns has been expanding more and more, but to keep this book easy to understand, we are going to focus only on those traditional personal pronouns. Spanish has slightly more personal pronouns than English.

Pronoun Translation Mode

Yo	Yoh	I	First-person singular
Tú	Too	You	Second person singular
Él	Ehl	He	Third-person singular
Ella	Eh-yah	She	Third-person singular
Eso	Eh-soh	It	Third-person singular
Nosotros	Noh-soh-trohs	We	First-person plural
Ustedes	Oos-teh-dehs	You	Second-person plural
Ellos	Eh-yohs	They	Third-person singular

There's another second person singular pronoun, and it's reserved for formal conversations. The pronoun is "usted," pronounced "oos-ted," and it has its own conjugations.

We'll explore pronouns with a couple of examples:

Yo tomo café sin azúcar.

Yoh toh-moh cah-feh seen ah-soo-cahr.

I drink coffee without sugar.

Ellos viven en este edificio.

Eh-yohs bee-behn ehn ehs-teh eh-dee-fee-seeoh.

They live in this building.

Ella ama comer galletas.

Eh-yah ah-mah coh-mehr gah-yeh-tahs.

She loves eating cookies.

Days of the Week

The days of the week are one of the most important topics in any language since it is impossible for us not to use them every day. The good thing is that the days of the week in Spanish are quite easy to learn, although we must know that, unlike English, the days of the week in Spanish do not have the first letter in capital letters. Unless we are starting a paragraph or a sentence, we must write the entire word in lowercase.

Day	Pronunciation	Translation
Lunes	Loo-nehs	Monday
Martes	Mahr-tehs	Tuesday
Miércoles	Mee-ehr-coh-lehs	Wednesday
Jueves	Hoo-eh-behs	Thursday
Viernes	Bee-ehr-nehs	Friday
Sábado	Sah-bah-doh	Saturday
Domingo	Doh-meen-goh	Sunday

Let's see a couple of examples:

El viernes es mi día favorito de la semana.

Ehl bee-ehr-nehs ehs mee dee-ah fah-boh-ree-toh deh lah seh-mah-nah.

Friday is my favorite day of the week.

El jueves es dos días después del martes.

Ehl hooeh-behs ehs dohs dee-ahs dehs-pooehs dehl mahr-tehs.

Thursday is two days after Tuesday.

Voy a la iglesia todos los domingos.

Boh-ee ah lah ee-gleh-see-ah toh-dohs lohs doh-meen-gohs.

I go to church every Sunday.

Related Definitions

These definitions that we are going to see next do not have so much to do with the days of the week but with expressions of time in which we refer to some moment of the day. In fact, we can say that these four words that we are going to learn next are even more used than the days of the week since we will always need them, no matter what type of conversation we are having.

Day Pronunciation Translation

Hoy	Oh-ee	Today
Mañana	Mahn-neeah-nah	Tomorrow
Ayer	Ah-yehr	Yesterday
Pasado mañana	Pah-sah-doh mahn-neeah-nah	Day After Tomorrow

Examples of uses for these terms:

Vamos a la playa mañana.

Bah-mohs ah lah plah-yah mahn-neeah-nah.

Let's go to the beach tomorrow.

Ayer comimos pescado.

Ah-yehr coh-mee-mohs pehs-cah-doh.

Yesterday we ate fish.

The Months of the Year

The months of the year are one of the first things that are learned when one begins the path of learning in another language. Although these are not difficult to learn, we must know in advance that most of the months have a very different pronunciation than how they are said in English, but some months like June, July, February, March, December, October, and November have a different pronunciation. slightly similar pronunciation.

This will help us memorize each of those months in a much faster and more efficient way:

Month	Pronunciation	Translation
Enero	Eh-neh-roh	January
Febrero	Feh-breh-roh	February
Marzo	Mahr-soh	March
Abril	Ah-breel	April
Mayo	Mah-yoh	May
Junio	Hoo-neeoh	June
Julio	Hoo-leeoh	July
Agosto	Ah-gohs-toh	August
Septiembre	Sehp-tee-ehm-breh	September
Octubre	Ohc-too-breh	October
Noviembre	Noh-bee-ehm-breh	November
Diciembre	Dee-see-ehm-breh	December

A couple of phrases of common use within months:

Mi cumpleaños es en diciembre.

Mee coom-pleh-ahn-neeohs ehs ehn dee-see-ehm-breh.

My birthday is in December.

¿Cuánto falta para marzo?

Cooahn-toh fahl-tah pah-rah mahr-soh

How long is it until March?

Yo salgo de vacaciones en julio.

Yoh sahl-goh deh bah-cah-seeoh-nehs ehn hoo-leeoh.

I go on vacation in July.

Verb Conjugation

As expected, verbs are one of the fundamental things to know when learning to speak a new language. Wanting to know a new language without learning the verbs is like starting to build a house starting from the roof, that is, it is simply impossible. That is why, below, we are going to see the correct forms in which each of the verbs must be conjugated, so that we know how to express ourselves when we speak using each of these verbs.

Regular verbs in Spanish are divided into three categories:

1. Those that end with "ar,"
2. Those that end with "er," and
3. Those that end with "ir."

These three groups of verbs have slightly different conjugation patterns, which is why it's important to divide them based on their last two letters. In this chapter we'll go over the three main conjugation patterns you'll use for verbs in the present tense.

It's important to point out that only regular verbs will follow this pattern. Irregular verbs, which won't be completely covered in this book, have different pronunciations. In any case, there's no better way to identify and learn the conjugation of irregular verbs than to read Spanish texts, so it's just a matter of time before you get the hang of it.

Verb That Ends With AR

We're going to use the example of the verb "amar" (to love).

Pronoun(s)	Conjugation	Pronunciation	Mode
Yo	Amo	Ah-moh	First-person singular
Tú	Amas	Ah-mahs	Second-person singular
Usted	Ama	Ah-mah	Second-person singular
Él/ Ella/ Eso	Ama	Ah-mah	Third-person singular
Nosotros	Amamos	Ah-mah-mohs	First-person plural
Ustedes	Aman	Ah-mahn	Second-person plural
Ellos / Ellas	Aman	Ah-mahn	Third-person plural

Verbs that End with "ER"

We will use the verb "correr" (to run).

Pronoun(s)	Conjugation	Pronunciation	Mode
Yo	Corro	Coh-rroh	First-person singular
Tú	Corres	Coh-rrehs	Second-person singular
Usted	Corre	Coh-rreh	Second-person singular
Él/ Ella/ Eso	Corre	Coh-rreh	Third-person singular
Nosotros	Corremos	Coh-rreh-mohs	First-person plural
Ustedes	Corren	Coh-rrehn	Second-person plural
Ellos/ Ellas	Corren	Coh-rrehn	Third-person plural

Verbs That End With "IR"

We will use the verb "vivir" (to live).

Pronoun(s)	Conjugation	Pronunciation	Mode
Yo	Vivo	Bee-boh	First-person singular
Tú	Vives	Bee-behs	Second-person singular
Usted	Vive	Bee-beh	Second-person singular
Él/ Ella/ Eso	Vive	Bee-beh	Third-person singular

Nosotros	Vivimos	Bee-bee-mohs	First-person plural
Ustedes	Viven	Bee-behn	Second-person plural
Ellos/ Ellas	Viven	Bee-behn	Third-person plural

Verb to Be

The Spanish language divides the English verb "to be" in two different verbs, "ser," and "estar." "Ser" means "to be" in a sense of identity and stable traits and situations, so it's used to express name, gender, nationality, among other permanent aspects.

Instead, "estar" also means "to be," but expressing a temporary situation, such as location, emotional state, mental state, among other temporary aspects. "Estar" is also the "to be" Spanish verb used to construct progressive time tenses.

"Ser" Simple Present Conjugation

Pronoun(s)	Conjugation	Pronunciation	Mode
Yo	Soy	Soh-ee	First-person singular
Tú	Eres	Eh-rehs	Second-person singular
Usted	Es	Ehs	Second-person singular
Él/ Ella/ Eso	Es	Ehs	Third-person singular

Nosotros	Somos	Soh-mohs	First-person plural
Ustedes	Son	Sohn	Second-person plural

Ellos/ Ellas Son Sohn Third-person plural.

"Estar" Simple Present Conjugation

Pronoun(s)	Conjugation	Pronunciation	Mode
Yo	Estoy	Ehs-toh-ee	First-person singular
Tú	Estás	Ehs-tahs	Second-person singular
Usted	Está	Ehs-tah	Second-person singular
Él/ Ella/ Eso	Está	Ehs-tah	Third-person singular
Nosotros	Estamos	Ehs-tah-mohs	First-person plural
Ustedes	Están	Ehs-tahn	Second-person plural
Ellos/ Ellas	Están	Ehs-tahn	Third-person plural

We'll illustrate the use of both verbs with a couple of examples:

Nosotros estamos cansados de comer arroz.

Noh-soh-trohs ehs-tah-mohs cahn-sah-dohs deh coh-mehr ah-rrohs.

We're tired of eating rice.

Ella es muy buena escritora.

Eh-yah ehs mooee booeh-nah ehs-cree-toh-rah.

She's a very good writer.

Mi mamá está en el odontólogo.

Mee mah-mah ehs-tah ehn ehl oh-dohn-toh-loh-goh.

My mom is at the dentist.

Yo soy un abogado.

Yoh soh-ee oon ah-boh-gah-doh.

I'm a lawyer.

Verb to Have

As with the verb "to be," the Spanish language divides the verb "to have" into two different verbs "haber" and "tener." Both verbs work for expressing duty and obligation, but "haber" is the one used for verb tenses conjugation, while "tener" is the one used to express possession.

Verb to Do

The Spanish equivalent of the verb "to do" is "hacer," and it's used the same way. This verb mainly expresses actions, as it happens with "to do," however, it's not used to construct questions or conjugate verb tenses.

"Hacer" Simple Present Conjugation

Pronoun(s)	Conjugation	Pronunciation	Mode
Yo	Hago	Ah-goh	First-person singular
Tú	Haces	Ah-sehs	Second-person singular
Usted	Hace	Ah-seh	Second-person singular
Él/ Ella/ Eso	Hace	Ah-seh	Third-person singular
Nosotros	Hacemos	Ah-seh-mohs	First-person plural
Ustedes	Hacen	Ah-sehn	Second-person plural
Ellos/ Ellas	Hacen	Ah-sehn	Third-person plural

Here you'll have a couple of examples of how this verb is used:

Juan hace la tarea todas las tardes.

Hooahn ah-seh lah tah-reh-ah toh-dahs lahs tahr-dehs.

Juan does the homework every afternoon.

Nosotros hacemos quince ejercicios por tarde de entrenamiento.

Noh-soh-trohs ah-seh-mohs keen-seh eh-her-see-seeohs pohr tahr-deh deh ehn-treh-nah-mee-ehn-toh.

We do fifteen exercises per training afternoon.

Él hace la cena mientras yo limpio la sala.

Ehl ah-seh lah seh-nah mee-ehn-trahs yoh leem-peeoh lah sah-lah.

He does dinner while I clean the living room.

Articles

As with English articles, Spanish articles are divided between definite and indefinite articles. As it was explained at the beginning of this chapter, Spanish articles change with the gender of the noun they're affecting. They're also altered by whether the noun is singular or plural.

Definite Articles

The English determinate article is "the," and its equivalents in Spanish are "lo," "la," "los," and "las," depending on the gender and number of the nouns.

Article	Pronunciation	Use
El	Ehl	Masculine singular
La	Lah	Feminine singular
Los	Lohs	Masculine plural
Las	Lahs	Feminine plural

Here are some examples of this:

Los perros.

Lohs peh-rrohs.

The dogs.

Las peras.

Lahs peh-rahs.

The pears.

El piano.

The piano.

La ardilla.

Lah ahr-dee-yah.

The squirrel.

However, even if the noun is feminine, you shall use a masculine article if the noun starts with a strong syllable.

El águila.

Ehl ah-gee-lah

The eagle.

Indefinite Articles

These would be the equivalents of the English words "a" and "an." The Spanish indefinite articles are "un," "una," "unos," and "unas."

Article	Pronunciation	Use
Un	Oon	Masculine singular
Una	Oo-nah	Feminine singular
Unos	Oo-nohs	Masculine plural
Unas	Oo-nahs	Feminine plural

We'll take a look at a couple of examples. As with the definite articles, masculine indefinite articles are to be used with feminine nouns that start with a strong vowel.

Un gato.

Oon gah-toh.

A cat.

Una lagartija.

Oo-nah lah-gahr-tee-hah.

A lizard.

Unos monos.

Oo-nohs moh-nohs.

Some monkeys.

Unas sardinas.

Oo-nahs sahr-dee-nahs.

Some herrings.

Un ábaco.

Oon ah-bah-coh.

An abacus.

Chapter Exercises

Eng/Spa Matching

Match these words in English with their equivalent terms in Spanish.

#	English Term	Letter	Spanish Term
1	Monday	A	Octubre
2	Today	B	Sábado
3	March	C	Eres
4	Would	D	Lunes
5	Am	E	Mañana
6	Church	F	Jardín
7	Saturday	G	Cumpleaños
8	Are	H	Junio

9	Birthday	I	El
10	The	J	Sería
11	October	K	Hoy
12	Glad	L	Soy
13	June	M	Marzo
14	Tomorrow	N	Iglesia
15	Garden	O	Alegra

Fill in the Blank

Answer the questions by filling in the blanks.

1. Are months in Spanish capitalized? ____
2. What's the definite article to be used with the word "puerta" (door) in singular?

   ____
3. What's the conjugation of the verb "to have" for the following sentence: "Ustedes

   _____ que hacer la tarea" (you have to do the homework).
4. How do you say the number 1,005? ____
5. What's the formal equivalent of "you" in Spanish? _____

Translation

Write the Spanish translation of these English phrases.

1. I'll go visit my grandmother next Friday.
2. I want you to hand me that pencil.
3. The eagle is a very large bird.
4. December is my favorite month of the year.
5. They're coming over this Monday.

Chapter 2– Answer Key

The answers for the Eng/Spa Matching exercises are the only ones that are strict. The other answers usually allow some freedom to adapt and rephrase the sentences as long as the core concept is intact.

Eng/Spa Matching

1:D, 2:K, 3:M, 4:J, 5:L, 6:N, 7: B, 8:C, 9:G, 10:I, 11:A, 12:O, 13:H, 14:E, 15:F

Fill in the Blank

1. No, they aren't.
2. La
3. Tienen
4. Mil cinco
5. Usted

Translation

1. Yo iré a visitar a mi abuela el próximo viernes.
2. Quiero que me pases ese lápiz.
3. El águila es un ave muy grande.
4. Diciembre es mi mes favorito del año.
5. Ellos van a venir este lunes.

Next, we are going to see a conversation that includes some of the topics that we have seen in this chapter. Of course, in this chapter, we saw some basic things that we should know whenever we are learning to speak a new language, and that is why we are going to see an informal conversation between two people so that we can see how to introduce each of these phrases and words to our regular conversations. I promise we will see this conversation in Spanish, and then we will see the English translation so that we can identify and learn to interpret each of the things that are being said.

In this way, not only will we learn new words and phrases, but we will also be able to practice reading in Spanish. It would be great if we read this conversation aloud so that it would also help us to practice our speaking and the correct way to pronounce each of those words. This is something that we are going to see in each of the chapters in order to strengthen the knowledge that we have acquired through each of the contents that we are learning. We must always remember that when we learn a new language, the key is always to practice as much as we can, otherwise, the effort we make will be in vain.

A Typical Conversation in Spanish

Juan: Voy a ir al juego de béisbol la semana que viene con mi papá

Kike: Me alegra mucho oír eso Juan, yo creo que también voy a ir a ese juego, aunque aún no estoy muy seguro. Estuve averiguando y los precios son un poco elevados, pero voy a intentar a ver si consigo alguna opción que sea barata.

Juan: Nosotros teníamos el mismo problema, todos los tickets que había estaban un poco caros. Lo que hicimos fue buscar algunas ofertas en internet y pudimos conseguir un precio especial.

Kike: Excelente, creo que también haré eso para así poder ir al juego con mi papá, es un gran fanatico del béisbol. Lo qué pasa es que el siempre tiene que trabajar los días de semana, pero lo intentaré convencer a ver si quiere ir al juego el sábado.

Juan: Nosotros pudimos comprar las entradas a 200 dólares, y la verdad es que considero que es un precio bastante alto. Sin embargo, mi papá se va de viaje el mes que viene y esta era nuestra última oportunidad de poder ir a un juego de béisbol.

Kike: ¿A qué parte se va tu papá de viaje? ¿Va por cuestiones de trabajo?

Juan: Si, va por cuestiones de trabajo dos semanas a México. Específicamente va a Guadalajara, ya que es allí en donde queda la empresa en la que trabaja.

Kike: He oído que México es un país bastante lindo, y que hay muchas cosas turísticas que son bastante interesantes y valen la pena conocer. Sin duda alguna tu papá se va a divertir muchísimo en México.

Juan: No me quedan dudas de que se va a divertir mucho. Lo único malo es que son aproximadamente 12 horas de viaje, y a mi papá no le gustan mucho los aviones porque le da miedo. Siempre prefiere viajar en carro o en bote.

Kike: Los aviones también me daban miedo cuando era niño, pero luego fui aprendiendo que hay muchas más posibilidades de tener un accidente en un carro o en un bote, así que no tengo dudas de que tu papá va a disfrutar mucho ese viaje.

Translation

Juan: I'm going to the baseball game next week with my dad.

Kike: I'm very happy to hear that Juan, I think I'm going to go to that game too, although I'm not sure yet. I've been researching and the prices are a bit high, but I'm going to try and see if I can find an option that is cheap.

Juan: We had the same problem, all the tickets that were available were a bit expensive. What we did was look for some deals on the internet and we were able to get a special price.

Kike: Great, I think I'll do that too so I can go to the game with my dad, who's a big baseball fan. What happens is that he always has to work on weekdays, but I will try to convince him to see if he wants to go to the game on Saturday.

Juan: We were able to buy the tickets for 200 dollars, and the truth is that I consider it to be quite a high price. However, my dad is going on a trip next month and this was our last chance to get to a baseball game.

Kike: Where is your dad going on a trip? Are you going for work reasons?

Juan: Yes, he goes to Mexico for two weeks for work reasons. Specifically, he goes to Guadalajara, since that is where the company where he works is located.

Kike: I've heard that Mexico is a pretty beautiful country and that there are many tourist things that are quite interesting and worth knowing. Without a doubt, your dad is going to have a lot of fun in Mexico.

Juan: I have no doubt that he is going to have a lot of fun. The only bad thing is that it's about a 12-hour drive, and my dad doesn't really like planes because they're scary. He always prefers to travel by car or by boat.

Kike: Planes also scared me when I was a child, but then I learned that there are many more chances of having an accident in a car or on a boat, so I have no doubt that your dad will enjoy that trip a lot.

CHAPTER 3:

SMALL TALK AND NORMAL CONVERSATIONS

Throughout this chapter, we are going to review all those things that we are going to need to carry out a daily conversation. In other words, in this section, we are going to cover all those things that are necessary to be able to speak and understand other people in a clear and fluid way. Without a doubt, there is nothing more uncomfortable than not being able to communicate the way we want because we don't know what the other person is saying or because we simply can't find ways to communicate. That is why this is probably the most important chapter of the book as we are going to learn things of daily use. Of course, the other chapters are also of great importance and all the contents included in these chapters are also necessary.

However, everything that we are going to see in this chapter is things that we will always need, regardless of the circumstances in which our conversation with another person takes place. This is because we are not only going to use all this knowledge in conversations, but it will also be useful when we do a reading in Spanish, watch a movie, listen to a song, a podcast, or anything else that requires our knowledge of the Spanish language. Best of all, most of these things can be learned easily, as long as we have the necessary level of discipline to learn all these things and practice them as many times as necessary since we must remember that if we do not take care of practically everything we learn then we are going to end up forgetting all that very quickly.

Ideally, we could have another person who also speaks Spanish in order to practice in a much more fluid way. However, we know that this is not always easy, so we are also going to review some of the ways in which we can practice all these topics that we will see below in our day-to-day. One of those simple ways to practice Spanish on a daily basis is by reading. We all know how wonderful books are and all the wisdom that we can acquire from each of them, however, when we read in Spanish we will also be learning many new words, grammatical structures, verbs, and many other things that will help us a lot in our learning process.

In the same way, we can listen to songs in Spanish, which will also help us a lot to understand the way in which Spanish speakers normally express themselves. Also, while we are learning we are going to be having fun and learning about a new culture. Finally, we can try watching a movie in Spanish. In this way, we will be able to put the subtitles in English, and thus understand each of the things that he is saying in the film. Of course, it will not be easy at first, but little by little we will get used to it and do it in a much more natural way. All these methods will help us to practice all the topics and contents that we are going to see in this chapter so that we can learn them perfectly.

Past Tense

We'll cover the preterite imperfect of the indicative conjugations, and the preterite indefinite of the indicative conjugations. The first group is used to describe past events that have no clear beginning or end; on the other hand, the second group is used for exactly the opposite.

These are terms related to the weather and its expressions:

Term	Pronunciation	Translation
Soleado	Soh-leh-ah-doh	Sunny
Lluvia	Yoo-beeah	Rain
Llovizna	Yoh-bees-nah	Drizzle
Granizo	Grah-nee-soh	Hail
Cálido	Cah-lee-doh	Warmth
Frío	Freeoh	Cold
Calor	Cah-lohr	Heat
Nublado	Noo-blah-doh	Cloudy
Tormenta	Tohr-mehn-tah	Storm
Trueno	Trooeh-noh	Thunder
Nevada	Neh-bah-dah	Snowfall

Here are some example phrases about weather:

Me gusta más el frío que el calor.

Meh goos-tah mahs ehl free-oh keh ehl cah-lohr.

I like the cold more than the heat.

Nos encantan los días nublados.

Nohs ehn-cahn-tahn lohs dee-ahs noo-blah-dohs.

We love cloudy days.

Él odia las tormentas.

Ehl oh-deeah lahs tohr-mehn-tahs.

He hates storms.

Colors

This may be one of the easiest topics to learn in the entire book since we only have to memorize them and there are no rules or grammatical structures to learn. In fact, we may already know some of these colors because we have heard them in a song, heard them on the radio, seen them in a magazine, or something similar. Of course, in order not to make this section tedious and pointless, we are only going to focus on the main colors, since they are the ones that we probably need to use in a sentence or in a conversation.

Color	Pronunciation	Translation
Rojo	Roh-hoh	Red
Azul	Ah-sool	Blue
Blanco	Blahn-coh	White
Negro	Neh-groh	Black
Verde	Behr-deh	Green
Amarillo	Ah-mah-ree-yoh	Yellow

Marrón	Mah-rrohn	Brown
Púrpura	Poor-poo-rah	Purple
Violeta	Beeoh-leh-tah	Violet
Rosado	Roh-sah-doh	Pink
Anaranjado	Ah-nah-rahn-hah-doh	Orange
Gris	Grees	Gray

With some examples of how to use these terms in Spanish:

El amarillo te queda muy bien.

Ehl ah-mah-ree-yoh teh keh-dah mooee bee-ehn.

Yellow suits you.

Mi bolso es el negro.

Mee bohl-soh ehs ehl neh-groh.

My bag is the black one.

Deberíamos pintar la casa de azul.

Deh-beh-ree-ah-mohs peen-tahr lah cah-sah deh ah-sool.

We should paint the house blue.

Presentations

Presentations are always going to be important in whatever language we are communicating in. This is because there will be many occasions where we arrive at places where we do not know anyone and we have to introduce ourselves. However, introducing ourselves is not just saying our names, but many times we also add extra information such as our age, our occupation, if we have children or partners, and all that. Similarly, there will be many occasions when the opposite happens. That is, there will be times when we have to ask someone else to introduce themselves so that we can get to know them better and learn more about that person.

That is why if we do not know how to express ourselves in terms of presentations, it will be very difficult for us to meet new people or to reach a place where we do not know anyone and function correctly. That's why we'll go over phrases we use when we want to present ourselves, to present someone else, or ask someone to present themselves.

Presenting Oneself

Saludos, mi nombre es Carlos.

Sah-loo-dohs mee nohm-breh ehs cahr-lohs.

Greetings, my name is Carlos.

Yo soy de Brasil.

Yoh soh-ee deh brah-seel.

I come from Brazil.

Yo tengo treinta años de edad.

Yoh tehn-goh treh-een-tah ahn-neeohs deh eh-dahd.

I am thirty years old

Yo soy un contador.

Yoh soh-ee oon cohn-tah-dohr.

I'm an accountant.

Yo estoy casado y tengo dos hijos.

Yoh ehs-toh-ee cah-sah-doh ee tehn-goh dohs hee-hos.

I'm married and have two kids.

Presenting Another Person

Saludos, él se llama Andrés.

Sah-loo-dohs ehl seh yah-mah ahn-drehs.

Greetings, his name is Andrés.

Él tiene veinticuatro años de edad.

Ehl tee-eh-neh beh-een-tee-cooah-troh ahn-neeohs deh eh-dahd.

He's twenty-four years old.

Él es un periodista.

Ehl ehs oon peh-reeoh-dees-tah.

He's a journalist.

Él viene de México.

Ehl bee-eh-neh deh meh-hee-coh.

He comes from México.

Él es soltero.

Ehl ehs sohl-teh-roh.

He's single.

Asking Someone to Present Themselves

¿Cómo te llamas?

Coh-moh teh yah-mahs

What's your name?

¿De dónde eres?

Deh dohn-deh eh-rehs

Where are you from?

¿Cuántos años tienes?

Cooahn-tohs ahn-neeohs tee-eh-nehs

How old are you?

¿Cuál es tu profesión?

Cooahl ehs too proh-feh-seeohn

What's your profession?

¿Estás casado o soltero?

Ehs-tahs cah-sah-doh oh sohl-teh-roh

Are you married or single?

Adjectives

Adjectives in Spanish work the same way as in English. The only real difference is that Spanish adjectives are concerned with the gender of the noun. They'll end with "a" if the noun is feminine and "o" if the noun is masculine.

Here's a simple list of common adjectives you'll probably be using in small talk:

Adjective	Pronunciation	Meaning
Feliz	Feh-lees	Happy
Triste	Trees-teh	Sad
Enojado	Eh-noh-hah-doh	Angry
Hambriento	Ahm-bree-ehn-toh	Hungry
Cansado	Cahn-sah-doh	Tired
Dormido	Dohr-mee-doh	Asleep
Despierto	Dehs-pee-ehr-toh	Awake
Malo	Mah-loh	Bad
Bueno	Boo-eh-noh	Good
Sencillo	Sehn-see-yoh	Plain
Guapo	Goo-ah-poh	Handsome
Hermoso	Ehr-moh-soh	Beautiful
Feo	Feh-oh	Ugly
Limpio	Leem-peeoh	Clean
Sucio	Soo-seeoh	Dirty
Ordenado	Ohr-deh-nah-doh	Tidy
Desordenado	Dehs-ohr-deh-nah-doh	Messy
Seco	Seh-coh	Dry
Mojado	Moh-hah-doh	Wet
Caliente	Cah-lee-ehn-teh	Hot
Fresco	Frehs-coh	Cool

Delicioso	Deh-lee-seeoh-soh	Delicious
Asqueroso	As-keh-roh-soh	Disgusting
Dulce	Dool-seh	Sweet
Salado	Sah-lah-doh	Salty
Amargo	Ah-mahr-goh	Bitter
Ácido	Ah-see-doh	Sour
Delgado	Dehl-gah-doh	Thin
Gordo	Gohr-doh	Fat
Alto	Ahl-toh	Tall
Bajo	Bah-hoh	Short
Pequeño	Peh-kehn-neeoh	Small
Grande	Grahn-deh	Big
Pesado	Peh-sah-doh	Heavy
Liviano	Lee-beeah-noh	Light
Lleno	Yeh-noh	Full
Vacío	Bah-seeoh	Empty
Rápido	Rah-pee-doh	Fast
Lento	Lehn-toh	Slow
Divertido	Dee-behr-tee-doh	Fun
Aburrido	Ah-boo-rree-doh	Boring

Possessive Adjectives

Spanish possessive adjectives work the same way as English possessive adjectives, so they replace words such as "my," "your," "his," "her," and so on. These would be the "atonic possessive adjectives," which are the most common ones and work exactly as adjectives. Besides the "atonic possessive adjectives," there are also "tonic possessive adjectives," which are written the same way as possessive pronouns, with the difference that tonic possessive adjectives are written next to the noun instead of replacing the noun altogether.

Atonic possessive adjectives are always written before the noun, while tonic possessive adjectives are written right after the noun. As with all adjectives, possessive adjectives end with an "a" or "o," depending on the gender of the object they're expressing possession of, they also add an "s" if the noun is plural.

Atonic Possessive Adjectives

Pronoun	Adjective	Pronunciation	Translation
Yo	Mi, Mis	Mee, Meehs	My
Tú	Tu, Tus	Too, Toos	Your
Usted	Su, Sus	Soo, Soos	Your
Él/ Ella/ Eso Su, Sus	Soo, Soos	His/ Her/ Its	
Nosotros	Nuestro, Nuestros	Nooehs-troh, Nooeh-strohs	Our
	Nuestra, Nuestras	Nooeh-strah, Nooeh-strahs	

| Ustedes | Su, Sus | Soo, Soos | Your |
| Ellos/ Ellas | Su, Sus | Soo, Soos | Your |

Tonic Possessive Adjectives

Pronoun	Adjective	Pronunciation
Yo	Mío, Míos	Meeoh, Meeohs
	Mía, Mías	Meeah, Meeahs
Tú	Tuyo, Tuyos	Too-yoh, Too-yohs
	Tuya, Tuyas	Too-yah, Too-yahs
Usted	Suyo, Suyos	Soo-yoh, Soo-yohs
	Suya, Suyas	Soo-yah, Soo-yahs
Él/ Ella/ Eso	Suyo, Suyos	Soo-yoh, Soo-yohs
	Suya, Suyas	Soo-yah, Soo-yahs
Nosotros	Nuestro, Nuestros	Nooehs-troh, Nooehs-trohs
	Nuestra, Nuestras	Nooehs-trah, Nooehs-trahs
Ustedes	Suyo, Suyos	Soo-yoh, Soo-yohs
	Suya, Suyas	Soo-yah, Soo-yahs
Ellos/ Ellas	Suyo, Suyos	Soo-yoh, Soo-yohs
	Suya, Suyas	Soo-yah, Soo-yahs

Here are some example phrases for the possessive adjectives:

Ellos siempre nos comparten su comida.

61

Eh-yohs see-ehm-preh nohs cohm-pahr-tehn soo coh-mee-dah.

They always share their food with us.

Yo cuido mucho a la novia mía.

Yoh cooee-doh moo-coh ah lah noh-beeah meeah.

I take care of my girlfriend.

Tú limpiabas tu casa todos los sábados.

Too leem-peeah-bahs too cah-sah toh-dohs lohs sah-bah-dohs.

You cleaned your house every Saturday.

Este perro tuyo es muy grande.

Ehs-teh peh-rroh too-yoh ehs mooee grahn-deh.

This dog of yours is too big.

Participle Verbs

Participle verbs are verbs used as adjectives. Instead of describing an action, they're adapted to speak about a quality of a noun, the same way an adjective does, and subjected to the same rules for adjectives: They change with the gender and number of the nouns. Participle verbs are conjugated in the past tense.

Here are a couple of examples that will make this concept easier to understand:

Los autos chocados se ven feos.

Lohs ah-oo-tohs choh-cah-dohs seh behn feh-ohs.

Crashed cars look ugly.

Me encantan las camisas teñidas.

Meh ehn-cahn-tahn lahs cah-mee-sahs tehn-nee-dahs.

I love dyed shirts.

Parts of the Body

As it happens in the case of colors, the parts of the body may not be the most common things to mention in an everyday conversation, but without a doubt some important ones that we learn the most important ones in order to be prepared for when the situation arises. chance.

Do not be scared, we are not going to review some parts of the body that can be very complicated or that are not entirely daily, since the important thing here is not to obtain a degree in medicine but to be able to learn some of the things that we are going to use on a daily basis in conversations, readings, when we watch a movie or any other situation that deserves it.

Word	Pronunciation	Translation
Cabeza	Cah-beh-sah	Head
Ojos	Oh-hos	Eyes
Nariz	Nah-rees	Nose
Orejas	Oh-reh-has	Ears
Cuero cabelludo	Cooeh-roh cah-beh-yoo-doh	Scalp
Cráneo	Crah-neh-oh	Skull
Boca	Boh-cah	Mouth
Dientes	Dee-ehn-tehs	Teeth
Lengua	Lehn-gooah	Tongue
Mandíbula	Mahn-dee-boo-lah	Jaw
Cuello	Cooeh-yoh	Neck

Hombros	Ohm-brohs	Shoulders
Pecho	Peh-choh	Chest
Corazón	Coh-rah-sohn	Heart
Pulmones	Pool-moh-nehs	Lungs
Brazo	Brah-soh	Arm
Codo	Coh-doh	Elbow
Mano	Mah-noh	Hand
Dedos	Deh-dohs	Fingers/ Toes
Espalda	Ehs-pahl-dah	Back
Abdomen	Ahb-doh-mehn	Abdomen
Panza	Pahn-sah	Belly
Estómago	Ehs-toh-mah-goh	Stomach
Hígado	Ee-gah-doh	Liver
Riñones	Reen-neeoh-nehs	Kidneys
Intestinos	Een-tehs-tee-nohs	Intestines/ Bowels
Trasero	Trah-sehr-oh	Ass
Piernas	Pee-ehr-nahs	Legs
Rodilla	Roh-dee-yah	Knee
Pies	Pee-ehs	Feet
Dolor	Doh-lohr	Pain
Duele	Dooeh-leh	Pains
Mareo	Mah-reh-oh	Dizzy

Fiebre	Fee-eh-breh	Fever
Tos	Tohs	Cough
Estornudo	Ehs-tohr-noo-doh	Sneeze

As usual, we'll go over a couple of examples:

Me duele el estómago.

Meh dooeh-leh ehl ehs-toh-mah-goh.

My stomach hurts.

Ayer tuve fiebre con tos y mareo.

Ah-yehr too-beh fee-eh-breh cohn tohs ee mah-reh-oh.

I had a fever yesterday with coughs and dizziness

Tengo dolor de cabeza.

Tehn-goh doh-lohr deh cah-beh-sah.

I have a headache.

Getting to Know Each Other

We'll explore some phrases that will be used when speaking about hobbies and things we like or dislike. Pay close attention to the words used to describe things like "gustar," love "amar ("encantar" is also used), dislike "desagradar" ("no me gusta" is also used), and so on.

Me gusta el fútbol.

Meh goos-tah ehl foot-bohl.

I like soccer.

¿Qué tipo de música escuchas?

Keh tee-poh deh moo-see-cah ehs-coo-chahs

What kind of music do you listen to?

¿Te gusta la música clásica?

Teh goos-tah lah moo-see-cah clah-see-cah

Do you like classical music?

A mi me gusta escuchar jazz.

Ah mee meh goos-tah ehs-coo-chahr yahs.

I like listening to jazz.

¿Cuál es tu equipo favorito?

Coo-ahl ehs too eh-kee-poh fah-boh-ree-toh

What's your favorite team?

Me encantan las películas románticas.

Meh ehn-cahn-tahn lahs peh-lee-coo-lahs roh-mahn-tee-cahs.

I love romantic movies.

¿Te gusta leer libros de terror?

Teh goos-tah leh-ehr lee-brohs deh teh-rrohr

Do you like to read horror books?

Me gusta ir a museos con mi pareja.

Meh goos-tah eer ah moo-seh-ohs cohn mee pah-reh-hah.

I like going to museums with my significant other.

Nos encanta salir a bailar juntos.

Nohs ehn-cahn-tah sah-leer ah bah-ee-lahr hoon-tohs.

We love going out to dance together.

A ellos les desagradan los clubes ruidosos.

Ah eh-yohs lehs deh-sah-grah-dahn lohs cloo-behs rooee-doh-sohs.

They dislike noisy clubs.

Ella es feliz siempre que puede ir a la playa.

Eh-yah ehs feh-lees see-ehm-preh keh pooeh-deh eer ah lah plah-yah.

She's happy as long as she can go to the beach.

Chapter Exercises

Eng/Spa Matching

Match these words in English with their equivalent terms in Spanish

#	English Term	Letter	Spanish Term
1	Black	A	Mío
2	Kidneys	B	Lengua
3	Nose	C	Riñones
4	Red	D	Azul

5	Teeth	E	Cuero cabelludo
6	Blue	F	Nariz
7	Tongue	G	Negro
8	Rain	H	Soleado
9	His	I	Dientes
10	Fingers	J	Rojo
11	Sunny	K	Codo
12	Scalp	L	Ojos
13	Mine	M	Lluvia
14	Elbow	N	Su
15	Eyes	O	Dedos

Fill in the Blank

Answer the question by filling in the blank.

1. What's the preterite indefinite conjugation of the verb "cantar" (to sing) in the first person singular and plural?

   ____

2. How do you ask someone to present themselves? ____
3. How would you say that the day is sunny? ____
4. What verb conjugation is the best fit for expressing situations with a clear starting point and ending point?

   ____

5. Which possessive adjectives are the same as possessive pronouns? ____

Translation

Write the Spanish translation of these English phrases.

1. I love dressing in black.
2. Nice to meet you, my name is Greg.
3. Sunny days like these are best for training.
4. I hope you enjoy my song.
5. Crops are thankful for rainy days.

Chapter 3– Answer Key

The answers for the Eng/Spa Matching exercises are the only ones that are strict. The other answers usually allow some freedom to adapt and rephrase the sentences as long as the core concept is intact.

Eng/Spa Matching

1:G, 2:C, 3:F, 4:J, 5:I, 6:D, 7:B, 8:M, 9:N, 10:O, 11:H, 12:E, 13:A, 14:K, 15:L

Fill in the Blank

1. Canté y cantamos.
2. Saludos ¿Cómo te llamas? ¿Te podrías presentar por favor?
3. El día está soleado.
4. Preterite indefinite.
5. Tonic possessive adjectives

Translation

1. Me encanta vestirme de negro.
2. Un placer conocerte, mi nombre es Greg.
3. Días soleados como estos son lo mejor para entrenar.
4. Espero que disfruten esta canción.
5. Los cultivos agradecen los días lluviosos.

En el capítulo anterior, vimos el ejemplo de una conversación cotidiana, que nos ayudó mucho a comprender todos los tópicos y contenidos que habíamos aprendido en ese capítulo. Para este nuevo capítulo, vamos a cambiar un poco la dinámica, ya que esta vez lo que vamos a hacer es un ejemplo ficticio en donde una persona se presenta y habla acerca de sí mismo. Esto se hace con el objetivo de que podamos ver un ejemplo de varios párrafos en un formato que incluya la mayoría de los contenidos y enseñanzas que hemos visto en este capítulo. Sin duda alguna, esto nos ayudará mucho a poder interpretar ciertas cosas y a que podamos tener mucha práctica a través de la lectura y de la pronunciación.

Como dijimos en el capítulo anterior, lo ideal es que leamos el siguiente párrafo en voz alta para que estemos practicando nuestro nivel de lectura en español, al igual que nuestro nivel de speaking, que son dos de los elementos más importantes cuando estamos aprendiendo un nuevo idioma. Esto nos va a permitir saber e identificar dónde podemos introducir cada una de las cosas que hemos ido aprendiendo a través de este capítulo para que así podamos tener un mejor nivel en nuestro español.

Presenting Pablo, a Student From Uruguay

¡Hola a todos! Mi nombre es Pablo. Nací en el año 1999 en Montevideo, capital de Uruguay. Sin embargo, durante los últimos tres años he estado viviendo en Inglaterra, ya que a mi papá lo transfirieron para trabajar en ese país hace algunos años. Mi infancia en Uruguay fue muy hermosa, ya que pude aprender todo acerca de esa maravillosa cultura y todas las ciudades bonitas que tiene.

Sin embargo, cuando tenía tres años, me tuve que mudar a Argentina, que es un país limítrofe con Uruguay, ya que mis papás creían que la economía sería mejor en ese país y que sería algo beneficioso para nosotros. Los primeros años viví en Buenos Aires, que es la capital de Argentina, pero luego me mudé a la ciudad de Rosario, que queda aproximadamente a una hora de Buenos Aires. En Rosario, todo era diferente, ya que las personas en Buenos Aires llevan un ritmo de vida mucho más rápido, se estresan mucho más fácilmente y suelen andar todo el tiempo preocupados. En cambio, en Rosario, todo era mucho más

71

tranquilo, ya que las personas vivían con más calma y era mucho más fácil hacer amigos.

Cuando me mudé a Inglaterra, las cosas fueron un poco difíciles para mi, ya que no sabía hablar inglés y tuve que adaptarme a una cultura totalmente nueva y que era muy distinta a la cultura en la cual yo había crecido. Actualmente vivo en la ciudad de Londres, tengo un carro azul y voy a la Universidad de Oxford en donde estudio economía. Mi sueño desde que era muy pequeño siempre ha sido el de ser un economista bastante reconocido a nivel mundial, y sé que a través del tiempo y con la acumulación de experiencia lo voy a poder lograr sin ningún problema.

Por supuesto, va a requerir de mucho esfuerzo y dedicación, pero nada en la vida es imposible siempre y cuando tengamos mucha motivación en lo que hacemos y tengamos una pasión enorme. Sin duda alguna, yo amo a la economía,y estoy seguro de que, en el fondo, la economía me ama a mi. Actualmente mi nivel de inglés es bastante bueno, y soy uno de los mejores alumnos de mi clase. Eso ha hecho que mi camino universitario sea mucho más fácil. A todas aquellas personas que están aprendiendo a hablar español, les digo que es algo fascinante, y así como yo pude aprender su idioma con mucho esfuerzo y dedicación, ustedes van a poder aprender el mio sin ningún problema. Sólo requiere de mucha constancia, disciplina y motivación.

Translation

Hello everyone! My name is Pablo. I was born in 1999 in Montevideo, the capital of Uruguay. However, for the last three years I have been living in England, as my dad was transferred to work in that country a few years ago. My childhood in Uruguay was very beautiful, since I was able to learn everything about that wonderful culture and all the beautiful cities that country has. However, when I was three years old, I had to move to Argentina, which is a country bordering Uruguay, since my parents believed that the economy would be better in that country and that it would be beneficial for us.

The first years I lived in Buenos Aires, which is the capital of Argentina, but then I moved to the city of Rosario, which is about an hour from Buenos Aires. In Rosario, everything was different, since people in Buenos Aires lead a much faster pace of life, they get stressed much more easily and tend to be worried all the time. On the other hand, in Rosario, everything was much calmer since people lived more calmly and it was much easier to make friends.

When I moved to England, things were a bit difficult for me as I couldn't speak English and I had to adapt to a totally new culture that was very different from the one I had grown up in. I currently live in the city of London, I have a blue car and I go to the University of Oxford where I study economics. My dream since I was very little has always been to be a world-renowned economist, and I know that over time and with the accumulation of experience I will be able to achieve it without any problem. Of course, it will require a lot of effort and dedication, but nothing in life is impossible as long as we are highly motivated in what we do and have enormous passion.

Without a doubt, I love the economy, and I am sure that, deep down, economy loves me. Currently my level of English is quite good, and I am one of the best students in my class. That has made my college journey so much easier. To all those people who are learning to speak Spanish, I tell you that it is something fascinating, and just as I was able to learn your language with a lot of effort and dedication, you will be able to learn mine without any problem. It just requires a lot of perseverance, discipline and motivation.

CHAPTER 4:

ADDRESSES AND TRAVELS

It does not matter if we are learning to speak Spanish for work reasons or because we simply like this language. One of the things that we must always learn when we want to speak another language is things related to travel and directions. Suppose we are going on a trip to Spain or to a country in South America, then we are going to need to know each of these things so that we never get lost and always get to the place we want quickly and easily. All these things are usually a bit more complex, but without a doubt, with a little practice, we will be able to learn each of these things without any problem.

Future Simple Conjugation

This is included in this chapter because often we'll be speaking in the future tense while planning our vacations, buying tickets, stating our intentions for the day, etc.

Spanish has a traditional way to express the future where the conjugation of the verb changes, without needing anything else; this conjugation pattern is the same for verbs that end with "ar," "er," or "ir." There's another way to express future actions, and it's by using "voy a" (going to) in present tense + the main verb in infinitive. Both are equivalent and it depends on the speaker.

Future Simple Conjugation of Verbs that End with "AR," "ER," or "IR"

Pronoun(s)	Conjugation	Pronunciation	Mode
Yo	Amaré	Ah-mah-reh	First-person singular
Tú	Amarás	Ah-mah-rahs	Second-person singular
Usted	Amará	Ah-mah-rah	Second-person singular
Él/ Ella/ Eso	Amará	Ah-mah-rah	Third-person singular
Nosotros	Amaremos	Ah-mah-reh-mohs	First-person plural
Ustedes	Amarán	Ah-mah-rahn	Second-person plural

Present Tense Conjugation of the Verb "Ir" (to go)

Pronoun(s)	Conjugation	Pronunciation	Mode
Yo	Voy	Boh-ee	First-person singular
Tú	Vas	Bahs	Second-person singular
Usted	Va	Bah	Second-person singular

Él/ Ella/ Eso	Va	Bah	Third-person singular
Nosotros	Vamos	Bah-mohs	First-person plural

We'll have a couple of future tense sentences to illustrate this:

El año que viene nos vamos a Francia.

Ehl ahn-neeoh keh bee-eh-neh nohs bah-mohs ah eer ah frahn-seeah.

Next year we're going to France.

Pronto viajaremos a Chile.

Prohn-toh beeah-hah-reh-mohs ah chee-leh.

Soon, we'll travel to Chile.

El jueves vamos a comer en un restaurante.

Ehl hooeh-behs bah-mohs ah coh-mehr ehn oon rehs-tah-oo-rahn-teh.

This Thursday we're going to eat in a restaurant.

Compraremos los boletos de avión cuando estén de oferta.

Cohm-prah-reh-mohs lohs boh-leh-tohs deh ah-beeohn cooahn-doh ehs-tehn deh oh-fehr-tah.

We'll buy the plane tickets when they're on sale.

Means of Transportation

One of the most important things that we must know, especially when we are going to travel, are the means of transport. No one would like to be in the country on vacation and not know how to get around because they don't know how to communicate. That is why in this section we are going to see some of the means of transport most used by society on a day-to-day basis, as well as the correct pronunciation that we should give each of them.

It is important to note that many of them have the same meaning but the same pronunciation since in Spanish there are many words that have the same meaning. The good thing is that each of these means of transport is easy to learn and pronounce, so we shouldn't have any problem learning about them.

Vehicle	Pronunciation	Translation
Automóvil	Ah-oo-toh-moh-beel	Car
Carro	Cah-rroh	Car
Coche	Coh-cheh	Car
Motocicleta	Moh-toh-see-cleh-tah	Motorcycle
Barco	Bahr-coh	Ship
Bote	Boh-teh	Boat
Avión	Ah-beeohn	Airplane
Caminar	Cah-mee-nahr	Walk

Here are some examples of common phrases with vehicles:

Necesitamos ir a un alquiler de automóviles.

Neh-seh-see-tah-mohs eer ah oon ahl-kee-lehr deh ah-oo-toh-moh-bee-lehs.

We need to go to a car rental.

Sólo se puede llegar a la isla por avión.

Soh-loh seh pooeh-deh yeh-gahr ah la h ees-lah pohr ah-beeohn.

You can only reach the island by plane.

Las motocicletas no están permitidas por aquí.

Lahs moh-toh-see-cleh-tahs noh ehs-tahn pehr-mee-tee-dahs pohr ah-kee.

Motorcycles are not allowed around here.

Creo que mi coche está averiado.

Creh-oh keh mee coh-cheh ehs-tah ah-beh-reeah-doh.

I believe my car has broken down.

Giving Directions

It is possible that being in any part of the world, any day of the week, we need to ask for an address, or on the contrary, someone who is lost asks us to give him an address. This can happen any day and at any time, so we must be prepared to know how to respond in each of these situations. Of course, many times when we are giving directions we will have to use the names of the stores, the parks, or the places we want to go, but it is important to know the grammatical structures on which we are going to give or ask for those directions.

If we don't learn these things, then we will always depend on applications like Google Maps, which is undoubtedly something that will limit us a lot in our lives. On the contrary, learning everything related to addresses will mean that we never have to depend on these things.

Asking for Directions

This is mostly done with the interrogative adverb "dónde" (where). Here are some example phrases that illustrate this:

¿Dónde está el hospital?

Dohn-deh ehs-tah ehl ohs-pee-tahl

Where's the hospital?

Giving Directions

We'll go over verbs and nouns related to directions, then we'll have a couple of example phrases to illustrate it.

Term	Pronunciation	Translation
Continuar	Cohn-tee-nooahr	To continue
Girar	Hee-rahr	To turn
Ir	Eer	To go
Avanzar	Ah-bahn-sahr	To advance
Tomar	Toh-mahr	To take
Derecho	Deh-reh-coh	Straight
Izquierda	Ess-kee-ehr-dah	Left
Derecha	Deh-reh-chah	Right
Atrás	Ah-trahs	Back
Norte	Nohr-teh	North
Sur	Soor	South
Este	Ehs-teh	East
Oeste	Oh-ehs-teh	West

Sigue derecho y cruza tres calles.

See-geh deh-reh-coh ee croo-sah trehs cah-yehs.

Go straight and cross after three streets.

El parque queda atrás del hospital.

Ehl pahr-keh keh-dah ah-trahs dehls ohspee-tahl.

The park is behind the hospital.

El lago está al oeste de la ciudad.

Ehl lah-goh ehs-tah ahl oh-ehs-teh deh lah seeoo-dahd.

The lake is West of the city.

El hospital queda a tres calles a la derecha de aquí.

Ehl ohs-pee-tahl keh-dah ah trehs kah-yehs ah lah deh-reh-chah deh ah-kee.

The hospital is three blocks to the right of here.

The Four Seasons

Relevant to holiday planning, this is how the four seasons are named in Spanish. As it happens with months and days of the week, the seasons in Spanish aren't capitalized.

Season	Pronunciation	Translation
Primavera	Pree-mah-beh-rah	Spring
Verano	Beh-rah-noh	Summer
Otoño	Oh-tohn-neeoh	Autumn/Fall
Invierno	Een-bee-ehr-noh	Winter

Here are a couple of example sentences that include seasons:

Los inviernos son demasiado fríos por aquí.

Lohs een-bee-ehr-nohs sohn deh-mah-seeah-doh free-ohs pohr ah-kee.

The winters are too cold around here.

Me gusta lo soleado que es el verano.

Meh goos-tah loh soh-leh-ah-doh keh ehs ehl beh-rah-noh.

I like how sunny the summer is.

Japón es hermoso en primavera.

Hah-pohn ehs ehr-moh-soh ehn pree-mah-beh-rah.

Japan is beautiful in spring.

Other Relevant Sentences

We'll go over important phrases that you should learn before going to a foreign country:

¿Dónde queda inmigración?

Dohn-deh keh-dah een-mee-grah-seeohn.

Where's immigration?

¿Qué hoteles hay en la zona?

Keh oh-teh-lehs ah-ee ehn lah soh-nah

What hotels are in the area?

Tiene hospedaje por 72 horas.

Tee-eh-neh ohs-peh-dah-heh pohr seh-tehn-tah ee dohs oh-rahrs.

Has lodging for 72 hours.

Vas a perder tu vuelo.

Bahs ah pehr-dehr too booeh-loh.

You're going to miss your flight.

¿Dónde está la piscina?

Dohn-deh ehs-tah lah pees-see-nah

Where's the pool?

Chapter Exercises

Eng/Spa Matching

Match these words in English with their equivalent terms in Spanish.

#	English Term	Letter	Spanish Term
1	Car	A	Vuelo
2	Winter	B	Primavera
3	Left	C	Verano
4	Where	D	Motocicleta
5	Flight	E	Derecho
6	Summer	F	Dónde
7	Ship	G	Invierno
8	Zone	H	Coche

9	Allowed	I	Piscina
10	Straight	J	Izquierda
11	Motorcycle	K	Permitido
12	College	L	Derecha
13	Pool	M	Barco
14	Right	N	Zona
15	Spring	O	Universidad

Fill in the Blank

Answer the questions by filling in the blanks.

1. How do you do the alternative future tense conjugation? ____

2. Name three ways to say "car" in Spanish. ____
3. What's the traditional future tense conjugation of the verb "vivir" (to live). ____
4. How do you say "turn left" in Spanish? ____
5. Are seasons capitalized in Spanish? ____

Translation

Write the Spanish translation of these English phrases.

1. It's better to call a cab so it can take us.
2. To reach the hospital you'll need to turn right on the next street and then go straight from there.
3. I enjoy sailing on large ships.
4. Riding a motorcycle makes me feel free.
5. My girlfriend loves taking pictures in the fall.

En este capítulo estuvimos enfocados en hablar de cosas muy elementales como los viajes y las cuestiones básicas que debemos saber al irnos de vacaciones y dar o recibir direcciones. Sin duda alguna, estos son tópicos súper importantes a la de hora de irnos de vacaciones, ya que es imposible estar en un país o en una ciudad que no conocemos si no sabemos la forma correcta de pedir y dar direcciones. Es por eso, que siguiendo lo que hemos hecho en capítulos anteriores, en donde hacíamos ejemplos de conversaciones o de algún monólogo, en este capítulo vamos a ver un pequeño artículo que nos va a hablar sobre algún destino turístico bastante conocido en Sudamérica. No sólo podremos reforzar nuestro nivel de lectura en español, sino que también podremos aprender un poco más acerca de otras culturas.

De esta manera, estaremos aprendiendo dos cosas a la misma vez. Recuerda que es muy importante que hagas la lectura en voz alta. Al principio, es normal que te cueste un poco, ya que es un idioma completamente nuevo, pero no te tienes que sentir apenado o algo por el estilo, ya que todos nos equivocamos durante este proceso de aprendizaje.

How Machu Picchu Was Built

Sin duda alguna, uno de los atractivos turísticos más grandes de Perú (y de toda Latinoamérica) es Machu Picchu, que es una zona que fue construida por los incas hace cientos de años, y que aún permanece intacta. Machu Picchu fue construida en la parte oriental de la Cordillera de los Andes, en la selva del Cusco. El increíble entorno natural que se encuentra a los alrededores de esta maravillosa ciudad inca no es la única razón por la que fue construida esa gran maravilla del mundo. Existen muchas teorías que tratan de explicar el porqué de la existencia de este monumento histórico de la humanidad. La mayoría de los expertos en geología e historia coinciden en que sirvió de puesto de control, centro agrícola, centro religioso y urbano.

A lo largo de los años, han habido muchas investigaciones en Machu Picchu que señalan que esta ciudad fue construida sobre una gran falla geológica, que tuvo como consecuencia principal la proliferación de bancos de piedra granítica, ideal para la edificación de esos maravillosos monumentos que podemos ver en internet (o si tenemos suerte, en vivo y en directo). Debido a eso, los incas construyeron los muros con una posición antisísmica, que ha logrado mantener el sitio sin mayores daños a lo largo de todos estos siglos.

Se dice que los incas construyeron sus principales ciudadelas en las partes elevadas e inaccesibles de las montañas, ya que así podrían tener una vista estratégica y privilegiada del entorno, al igual que se podían acercar a sus dioses celestiales, que debemos recordar eran muy importantes para ese tipo de tribus indígenas. Así como Machu Picchu, los incas edificaron otras ciudades en las altas montañas como por ejemplo: Sacsayhuaman, Pisac,

Ollantaytambo, Choquequirao, etc. Machu Picchu también es conocido como 'Ciudad en las nubes' puesto que está situado en una montaña alta y rodeada de un bosque nuboso. Su ubicación privilegiada les permitió a sus habitantes observar los fenómenos astronómicos con gran claridad.

Estas estructuras fueron ideales para la observación astronómica y así predecir los ciclos del sol durante la siembra y cosecha de productos agrícolas. El Intihuatana, por ejemplo, indica la fecha exacta de los solsticios, equinoccios y otros eventos astronómicos importantes. Sin duda alguna, esto nos habla de lo avanzada que eran esas tribus, y de la importancia que le daban al diseño arquitectónico de cada una de sus ciudades. Muchas veces las construcciones de hoy en día sólo tienen los costos y las cuestiones relacionadas a los tiempos de construcción, pero en aquel entonces, era muy importante darle una estructura arquitectónica hermosa a cada una de las obras que realizaban estas tribus.

Translation

Without a doubt, one of the biggest tourist attractions in Peru (and in all of Latin America) is Machu Picchu, which is an area that was built by the Incas hundreds of years ago, and that still remains intact. Machu Picchu was built in the eastern part of the Andes Mountains, in the jungle of Cusco. The incredible natural environment that surrounds this wonderful Inca city is not the only reason why this great wonder of the world was built. There are many theories that try to explain the reason for the existence of this historical monument of humanity. Most experts in geology and history agree that it served as a checkpoint, agricultural center, religious and urban center.

Over the years there have been many investigations in Machu Picchu that indicate that this city was built on a great geological fault, which had as its main consequence the proliferation of granite stone benches, ideal for the construction of those wonderful monuments that we can see on the internet (or if we're lucky, live and direct). Due to this, the Incas built the walls with an anti-seismic position, which has managed to maintain the site without major damage throughout all these centuries.

It is said that the Incas built their main citadels in the high and inaccessible parts of the mountains since that way they could have a strategic and privileged view of the environment, just as they could get closer to their celestial gods, which we must remember were very important. for that type of indigenous tribe. As well as Machu Picchu, the Incas built other cities in the high mountains such as: Sacsayhuaman, Pisac, Ollantaytambo, Choquequirao, etc. Machu Picchu is also known as 'City in the clouds' since it is located on a high mountain and surrounded by a cloud forest. Its privileged location allowed its inhabitants to observe astronomical phenomena with great clarity.

These structures were ideal for astronomical observation and thus predict the cycles of the sun during the planting and harvesting of agricultural products. The Intihuatana, for example, indicates the exact date of the solstices, equinoxes, and other important astronomical events. Without a doubt, this tells us how advanced these tribes were, and the importance they gave to the architectural design of each of their cities. Many times today's constructions only have costs and issues related to construction times, but back then, it was very important to give a beautiful architectural structure to each of the works carried out by these tribes.

CHAPTER 5:

HOUSEHOLD, FOOD, AND SHOPPING

In all daily conversations we will find ourselves talking about things related to the home, food, and of course, the various purchases that we can make during the week. That is why it is extremely necessary that we know how to use the correct expressions to refer to all these kinds of things since we will always use them. It does not matter if we are talking to a friend, a family member, or even a stranger, since in the same way, these types of topics are always present in any type of formal or informal conversation that we carry out. Of course, most of what we are going to look at in this chapter have to do with specific words, and not with grammatical structures or some sentence rules.

In other words, to be able to use all the phrases and words that we are going to learn next, you must master all the content that we have been learning throughout the three previous chapters. Therefore, if we are still not sure that we have perfectly mastered any of the previous chapters or sections, we must review them again so that we can understand this chapter correctly. We must always remember that many times the contents that we are learning can be easily forgotten, so it is always important to practice them and review them as many times as necessary so that we can ensure that all these contents will remain engraved in our heads in the long term, which is the goal that all of us have.

Pricing

If we are learning to speak Spanish for work reasons, without a doubt this is a very important section for us. This is because in this section we are going to learn some of the most important terms in relation to financial, economic, and cost factors. This is something vital that we must know to carry out most of the works, for which it is important that we pay close attention to all the terms that we are going to learn next, as well as the various examples that we are going to review.

Of course, let's not be scared, because if we are not learning to speak Spanish for work reasons but more for tourism or a matter of personal growth, this section will also be very useful to us. We all need to ask the price of something before buying it, as well as knowing terms related to tariffs and taxes since they are very important when we are going to a city or country as tourists. That is why this section may seem a bit simple, but it is undoubtedly much more important than it seems since it is possible that we are going to use each of these terms a lot. We'll go over some terms that are important to study value and ask about the cost of items in stores; and then, as always, we'll cover a couple of phrases to illustrate this.

Term	Pronunciation	Translation
Precio	Preh-seeoh	Price
Costo	Cohs-toh	Cost
Cuesta	Cooehs-tah	Cost
Valor	Bah-lohr	Value
Vale	Bah-leh	Values

Este pantalón vale doscientos.

Ehs-teh pahn-tah-lohn bah-leh dohs-see-ehn-tohs.

These pants are worth two hundred.

El precio por mis servicios es de veinte la hora.

Ehl preh-seeoh pohr mees sehr-bee-seeohs ehs deh beh-een-teh lah oh-rah.

The price for my services is twenty per hour.

Appreciating Food

When we talk about food, it is impossible not to use adjectives, since we will always need them to describe how good or how bad the food was. That is, adjectives help us describe how our experience has been after having eaten something, whether we have prepared it ourselves or it is food from a restaurant. As we all know, it is normal that when we are in a city or a country as tourists, we eat in many restaurants and try a lot of new food, since that is one of the most wonderful experiences of traveling and learning about other cultures. Knowing each of these adjectives and expressions will help us communicate much better when we are eating in a restaurant, or simply when we are going to eat with a friend or family member.

Of course, we can describe how the food was with many other adjectives, which will vary especially depending on the country we are in. However, below we are going to see some of the most common adjectives and terms that we are going to use on a daily basis when we are going to refer to food. We'll go over some words and phrases used when we want to rate the food and express gratitude for it.

Term	Pronunciation	Translation
Delicioso	Deh-lee-seeoh-soh	Delicious
Rico	Ree-coh	Rich, tasty
Sabroso	Sah-broh-soh	Tasty
Salado	Sah-lah-doh	Salty
Dulce	Dool-seh	Sweet
Sour	Soh-oor	Agrio
Amargo	Ah-mahr-goh	Bitter
Sabor	Sah-bohr	Taste
Textura	Tex-too-rah	Texture

Mi sopa está rica, pero demasiado caliente.

Mee soh-pah ehs-tah ree-cah peh-roh deh-mah-seeah-doh cah-lee-ehn-teh.

My soup is good but way too hot.

Me encanta la textura de la nieve.

Meh ehn-cahn-tah lah tex-too-rah deh lah nee-eh-beh.

I love the texture of the snow.

Me encantan las cerezas dulces y amargas.

Meh ehn-cahn-tahn lahs seh-reh-sahs dool-sehs ee ah-mahr-gahs.

I love bitter and sweet cherries.

Food Items

The goal of this section is for us to learn the correct way in which we should pronounce some of the main foods that we are likely to interact with every day. In other words, in this chapter, we are going to learn about the main fruits, the most common drinks, some proteins, and everything related to the basic and most consumed foods in general. Of course, everyone has different tastes and it is possible that some of the foods that we are going to mention below may not be part of our daily diet, but in the same way, we are going to review them so that we can identify them quickly and simply in any store, market, restaurant or simply in any conversation in which any of these topics arise.

Here's a simple list of food items for every home:

Item	Pronunciation	Translation
Manzanas	Mahn-sah-nahs	Apples
Naranjas	Nah-rahn-has	Oranges
Cerezas	Seh-reh-sahs	Cherries
Fresas	Freh-sahs	Strawberries

Carne	Cahr-neh	Meat
Cerdo	Sehr-doh	Pork
Agua	Ah-gooah	Water
Pollo	Poh-yoh	Chicken
Harina	Ah-ree-nah	Flour
Maíz	Mah-ees	Corn
Champiñones	Cham-peen-neeoh-nehs	Mushrooms
Limón	Lee-mohn	Lemon
Melón	Meh-lohn	Melon
Jalea	Hah-leh-ah	Jam
Mantequilla de maní	Mahn-teh-kee-yah deh mah-nee	Peanut butter
Azúcar	Ah-soo-cahr	Sugar
Huevos	Oo-eh-bohs	Eggs
Arroz	Ah-rrohs	Rice
Pasta	Pahs-tah	Pasta
Pan	Pahn	Bread
Tomate	Toh-mah-teh	Tomato
Cebolla	Seh-boh-yah	Onion
Lechuga	Leh-choo-gah	Lettuce
Perejil	Peh-reh-heel	Parsley
Leche	Leh-cheh	Milk

Queso	Keh-soh	Cheese
Jamón	Hah-mohn	Ham
Salsa	Sahl-sah	Sauce
Papa	Pah-pah	Potatoe
Zanahoria	Sah-nah-oh-reeah	Carrot
Repollo	Reh-poh-yoh	Cabbage
Salsa de tomate	Sahl-sah deh toh-mah-teh	Ketchup
Mayonesa	Mah-yoh-neh-sah	Mayonnaise
Mostaza	Mohs-tah-sah	Mustard
Pimienta	Pee-mee-ehn-tah	Pepper
Sal	Sahl	Salt

We'll go over a couple of sentences with food items:

Me gustan los huevos con sal y pimienta.

Meh goos-tahn lohs ooeh-bohs cohn sahl ee pee-mee-ehn-tah.

I like eggs with salt and pepper.

Mi mamá cocina muy bien el cerdo.

Mee mah-mah coh-see-nah mooee bee-ehn ehl sehr-doh.

My mother cooks the pork very well.

Ella prefiere comer pasta antes que arroz.

Eh-yah preh-fee-eh-reh coh-mehr pahs-tah ahn-tehs keh ah-rrohs.

She prefers to eat pasta rather than rice.

Shopping

Without a doubt, one of the things that identify us all equally, regardless of our tastes or preferences, is that all of us must make purchases in our day to day, since we must go to the pharmacy, to the supermarket, to the hardware store or any other store to buy the things we need for our daily routine at home. Therefore, when we go on a trip or we are doing tourism, we must also know how to express ourselves regarding these situations, since we will always need to go shopping, whatever the specific circumstances that arise that day.

In the same way, each of these phrases and words is usually very common in people's daily conversations. So, this section will also help us identify each of those things so that we can carry out communication and conversation. much more fluid.

Here's a list of various types of stores and phrases that are relevant to shopping:

Types of Stores

Store	Pronunciation	Translation
Farmacia	Fahr-mah-seeah	Drugstore
Ferretería	Feh-rreh-teh-ree-ah	Hardware store
Mercado	Mehr-cah-doh	Market
Supermercado	Soo-pehr-mehr-cah-doh	Supermarket
Panadería	Pah-nah-deh-ree-ah	Bakery
Floristería	Floh-rees-teh-ree-ah	Flower store

| Tienda | Tee-ehn-dah | Store |
| Restaurante | Rehs-tah-oo-rahn-teh | Restaurant |

Relevant Phrases

Necesito llegar al mercado más cercano.

Neh-seh-see-toh yeh-gahr ahl mehr-cah-doh mahs sehr-cah-noh.

I need to get to the closest market.

¿Tiene vuelto de cien?

Tee-eh-neh booehl-toh deh see-ehn

Do you have change for a 100 bill?

¿Cuánto le debo?

Cooahn-toh leh deh-boh

How much do I owe you?

No lo quiero, no me gusta.

Noh loh kee-eh-roh noh meh goos-tah.

I don't want it; I don't like it.

¿Aceptan crédito?

Ah-sehp-tahn creh-dee-toh

Do you accept credit?

¿Esto viene con garantía?

Ehs-toh bee-eh-neh cohn gah-rahn-tee-ah

Does this come with a warranty?

Necesito comprar regalos para mi familia. ¿Dónde consigo una tienda de regalos?

Neh-seh-see-toh cohm-prahr reh-gah-lohs pah-rah mee fah-mee-leeah dohn-deh cohn-see-goh oo-nah tee-ehn-dah deh reh-gah-lohs

I need to buy gifts for my family. Where shall I find a gift shop?

Vamos a la panadería que tienen muestras gratis.

Bah-mohs ah lah pah-nah-deh-ree-ah keh tee-eh-nehn mooehs-trahs grah-tees.

Let's go to the bakery, they have free samples.

¿En qué talla necesita?

Ehn keh tah-yah neh-seh-see-tah

What size do you need?

Me gusta este modelo, ¿lo tienen en verde?

Meh goos-tah ehs-teh moh-deh-loh loh tee-eh-nehn ehn behr-deh

I like this model, do you have it in green?

Hoy tenemos rebajas en la tienda.

Oh-ee teh-neh-mohs reh-bah-has ehn lah tee-ehn-dah.

Today we have sales in the store.

Home

Another of the topics that we undoubtedly have to learn about is everything related to real estate. This is something basic that we have to learn when we are starting to speak a language, since it does not matter if it is for work, curiosity, tourism or anything else, we will always need this set of words when we carry out a conversation, for more indifferent than it seems at first. That is why in this section we are going to see some of the most important concepts related to real estate and everything that has to do with the objects that we find in our homes.

Types of Homes

Home Pronunciation

Casa Cah-sah
Apartamento Ah-pahr-tah-mehn-toh
Mansión Mahn-seeohn
Cabaña Cah-bahn-neeah

Objects in the Living Room

Object	Pronunciation	Translation
Sofá	Soh-fah	Couch
Mesa	Meh-sah	Table
Butaca	Boo-tah-cah	Armchair
Alfombra	Ahl-fohm-brah	Carpet
Escritorio	Ehs-cree-toh-reeoh	Desk
Biblioteca	Bee-bleeoh-teh-cah	Library
Chimenea	Chee-meh-neh-ah	Chimney
Escultura	Ehs-cool-too-rah	Sculpture
Pintura	Peen-too-rah	Painting

Candelabro	Cahn-deh-lah-broh	Candelabra
Lámpara de techo	Lahm-pah-rah deh teh-choh	Ceiling lamp
Silla	See-yah	Chair
Televisión	Teh-leh-bee-seeohn	Television

Objects in the Bedroom

Object	Pronunciation	Translation
Cama	Cah-mah	Bed
Litera	Lee-teh-rah	Bunk bed
Ropero	Roh-peh-roh	Wardrobe
Armario	Ahr-mah-reeoh	Closet
Mesa	Meh-sah	Table
Espejo	Ehs-peh-hoh	Mirror
Tocador	Toh-cah-dohr	Dresser
Cortinas	Cohr-tee-nahs	Curtains
Sábana	Sah-bah-nah	Sheet
Almohadas	Ahl-moh-ah-dahs	Pillows
Lámpara	Lahm-pah-rah	Lamp
Computadora	Cohm-poo-tah-doh-rah	Computer
Escritorio	Ehs-cree-toh-reeoh	Desk

Objects in the Dining Room

Object	Pronunciation	Translation
Mesa	Meh-sah	Table
Sillas	See-yahs	Chairs
Alfombra	Ahl-fohm-brah	Carpet
Platos	Plah-tohs	Dishes
Vasos	Bah-sohs	Glasses
Jarra	Hah-rrah	Jar
Cubiertos	Coo-bee-ehr-tohs	Cutlery

Objects in the Bathroom

Object	Pronunciation	Translation
Ducha	Doo-chah	Shower
Bañera	Bahn-nee-eh-rah	Bathtub
Lavamanos	Lah-bah-mah-nohs	Sink
Espejo	Ehs-peh-hoh	Mirror

Objects in the Kitchen

Object	Pronunciation	Translation
Refrigerador	Reh-free-heh-rah-dohr	Fridge
Lavaplatos	Lah-blah-plah-tohs	Sink

Lavadora	Lah-bah-doh-rah	Washing machine
Lavavajillas	Lah-bah-bah-hee-yahs	Dishwasher
Grifo	Gree-foh	Tap
Horno microondas	Ohr-noh mee-croh-ohn-dahs	Microwave
Horno	Ohr-noh	Oven
Licuadora	Lee-cooah-doh-rah	Blender
Gabinetes	Gah-bee-nehts	Cabinets
Tostadora	Tohs-tah-doh-rah	Toaster
Estufa	Ehs-too-fah	Stove

Objects in the Garage

Object	Pronunciation	Translation
Lámpara	Lahm-pah-rah	Lamp
Automóvil	Ah-oo-toh-moh-beel	Car
Cobertizo	Coh-behr-tee-soh	Shed
Tanque de agua	Tahn-keh deh ah-gooah	Water tank

Objects in the Garden

Object	Pronunciation	Translation
Piscina	Pees-see-nah	Pool
Estanque	Ehs-tahn-keh	Pond
Árbol	Ahr-bohl	Tree
Fuente	Fooehn-teh	Fountain
Casa del perro	Cah-sah dehl peh-rroh	Doghouse
Pala	Pah-lah	Shovel
Manguera	Mahn-gueh-rah	Hose

Phrases for Eating

In this section, we are going to see some of the most important and common words and phrases that we are going to need when we want to express something related to eating or food in general. That is, these are the words that we are going to use when we want to say that we want to eat, that we want to see the restaurant menu, that we want to go eat at a specific place, and all those things. Each of these phrases is going to have great importance since we are going to need them whenever we go out to eat with friends, family, at home, or in a restaurant.

Similarly, it is likely that many times, in everyday conversations, we use some of these phrases to refer to something we ate or some gastronomic experience we have had. Without a doubt, learning all these things will help us a lot to expand our vocabulary in

Spanish and to know how we should develop a conversation at certain times.

Tengo hambre, quiero comer.

Tehn-goh ahm-breh kee-eh-roh coh-mehr.

I'm hungry, I want to eat.

Me gustaría ver el menú, por favor.

Meh goos-tah-ree-ah behr ehl meh-noo pohr fah-bohr.

I'd like to see the menu, please.

Me gustaría comer pizza.

Meh goos-tah-ree-ah coh-mehr pee-sah.

I'd like to eat pizza.

La cuenta, por favor.

Lah cooehn-tah pohr fah-bohr.

The check, please.

Quiero comer ensalada con mi pollo frito.

Kee-eh-roh coh-mehr ehn-sah-lah-dah cohn mee poh-yoh free-toh.

I'd like to have a salad with my fried chicken.

Esta comida está un poco cruda.

Ehst-ah coh-mee-dah ehs-tah oon poh-coh croo-dah.

This meal is a little bit raw.

Sólo puedo comer productos sin azúcar.

Soh-loh pooeh-doh coh-mehr proh-dooc-tohs seen ah-soo-cahr.

I can only eat sugar-free products.

Prueba un poco de esto.

Prooeh-bah oon poh-coh deh ehs-toh.

Have a taste of this.

Chapter Exercises

Eng/Spa Matching

Match these words in English with their equivalent terms in Spanish.

#	English Term	Letter	Spanish Term
1	Costs	A	Valor
2	Apples	B	Panadería
3	Market	C	Cuesta
4	Bathroom	D	Manzanas
5	Library	E	Tienda
6	Value	F	Farmacia

7	Bakery	G	Cebolla
8	Pork	H	Agua
9	Basement	I	Mercado
10	Mushrooms	J	Cerdo
11	Onion	K	Cocina
12	Drugstore	L	Baño
13	Kitchen	M	Champiñones
14	Store	N	Sótano
15	Water	O	Biblioteca

Fill in the Blank

Answer the questions by filling in the blanks.

1. How would you say that you're hungry in Spanish? ____
2. Name five objects in Spanish that you would find in most bedrooms._____
3. What does it mean if a Spanish store clerk tells you "estamos de oferta!"? ____
4. How would you ask for the price of a pair of shoes in Spanish? ____
5. How would you ask for the bill at a restaurant in Spanish? ____

Translation

Write the Spanish translation of these English phrases.

1. My kitchen has a sharp set of knives that I love to use every day.
2. My brother's bedroom is very tidy, he's an organized person.
3. All families should spend time together in the living room, even if it's just watching TV.
4. I loved the sweet and sour flavors of this cream pie!
5. My family loves it when I cook pasta with mushrooms.

Chapter 5– Answer Key

The answers for the Eng/Spa Matching exercises are the only ones that are strict. The other answers usually allow some freedom to adapt and rephrase the sentences as long as the core concept is intact.

Eng/Spa Matching

1:C, 2:D, 3:I, 4:L, 5:O, 6:A, 7:B, 8:J, 9:N, 10:M, 11:G, 12:F, 13:K, 14:E, 15:H

Fill in the Blank

1. Tengo mucha hambre.
2. In this case, the list is long, but you should name at least five of the following: cama, armario, mesa, lámpara, espejo, ropero, tocador, cortinas, sábana, almohadas, litera, etc.
3. It means that they're on sale.
4. ¿Cuánto cuesta ese par de zapatos?
5. Mesero, la cuenta, por favor.

Translation

1. Mi cocina tiene un lote de cuchillos afilados que me encanta usar todos los días.
2. La habitación de mi hermano está muy ordenada, él es una persona organizada.
3. Todas las familias deberían pasar tiempo juntos en la sala de estar, al menos si están viendo televisión como mínimo.
4. Yo amé los sabores dulces y agrios de este pie de crema.
5. A mi familia le encanta cuando cocino pasta con champiñones.

Al igual que hemos hecho en los capítulos anteriores, a continuación vamos a ver un artículo que nos explica un poco sobre cómo debemos ordenar nuestra casa para que esta sea mucho más espaciosa. De esta forma, no solo vamos a tener todo ordenado, sino que también vamos a poder contar con mucho más espacio y conseguir todas nuestras cosas de una forma más rápida. Por supuesto, la idea no es enseñar una lección de vida, sino que podamos obtener un poco de práctica al leer y hablar en voz alta un artículo entero en español.

How to Keep our house in Order

Una de las cosas que nos hace estar cómodos en nuestro hogar, sintiéndonos relajados, libres de estrés y también más felices, es tener nuestra casa limpia y recogida. Sin embargo, lograrlo no es fácil para todo el mundo, ya que a veces las personas no saben cómo llevar un orden en la casa, no pueden organizar sus cosas, o simplemente les parece algo demasiado fastidioso. Una de las primeras cosas que deberíamos hacer es deshacernos de todas aquellas cosas que no usamos ya que las consideramos como inservibles. A veces tenemos en nuestra casa un montón de cosas que no usamos o que ya no necesitamos, incluso es habitual encontrarnos con cosas que ni siquiera nos son útiles porque ya no funcionan.

Tendemos a guardar mucha "basura" que nos quita espacio para guardar las cosas realmente importantes. De igual manera, siempre se recomienda que cuando decidamos ordenar nuestra casa debemos hacerlo en el menor tiempo posible ya que así las posibilidades de éxito serán mayores debido a que estaremos más motivados durante todo el proceso. Si por el contrario ordenamos hoy una parte y dejamos el resto para dentro de varios días, esto puede hacer que vayamos retrasando la tarea hasta llegar incluso a no completarla.

Otra de las cosas que nos puede ayudar mucho (aunque ya eso pertenece a la etapa previa a mudarnos a nuestra casa), es tener muebles a medida. Tener una casa con muebles a medida nos va a ayudar mucho a aprovechar mejor todos los rincones de la casa. Aprovechar un rincón para poner una estantería o una repisa nos proporcionará más espacio de almacenaje. No obstante, debemos de tener cuidado de no cargar demasiado los espacios ya que no nos ayudan a liberarnos del estrés y tampoco ayudará a que posteriormente mantengamos el orden y la limpieza. Una vez que hemos ordenado nuestra casa, el trabajo que tenemos por delante es de mantenimiento.

De nada sirve todo el esfuerzo realizado en organizar la casa si a los tres días todo va a estar de nuevo patas arriba. Lo que ocurre con muchas personas es que limpian la casa el sábado o el domingo, pero después se pasan la semana entera desordenando o ensuciando. Sin duda alguna, el orden depende solamente de nosotros, así que debemos tener mucho más cuidado con nuestros hábitos y nuestra higiene alrededor de la casa.

Translation

One of the things that makes us feel comfortable in our home, feeling relaxed, stress-free, and also happier, is having our house clean and tidy. However, achieving this is not easy for everyone, since sometimes people do not know how to keep order in the house, they cannot organize their things, or it simply seems too annoying. One of the first things we should do is get rid of all those things that we do not use since we consider them useless. Sometimes we have a lot of things in our house that we do not use or that we no longer need, it is even common to find things that are not even useful to us because they no longer work.

We tend to keep a lot of "junk" that takes away space to store the really important things. In the same way, it is always recommended that when we decide to tidy up our house we should do it in the shortest time possible since this way the chances of success will be greater because we will be more motivated throughout the process. If, on the other hand, we order a part today and leave the rest for several days, this can cause us to delay the task until we even fail to complete it.

Another thing that can help us a lot (although that already belongs to the stage prior to moving into our house), is having custom-made furniture. Having a house with custom furniture will help us a lot to make better use of every corner of the house. Taking advantage of a corner to put a shelf or a shelf will provide us with more storage space. However, we must be careful not to load the spaces too much since they do not help us to free ourselves from stress and neither will it help us to maintain order and cleanliness later. Once we have tidied up our house, the job ahead of us is maintenance.

All the effort made in organizing the house is useless if after three days everything is going to be upside down again. What happens with many people is that they clean the house on Saturday or Sunday, but then they spend the whole week messing or dirty. Without a doubt, the order depends only on us, so we must be much more careful with our habits and our hygiene around the house.

CHAPTER 6:

BUSINESS, WORK, AND RELATIONSHIPS

As we said at the beginning of this book, there are many people who want to learn to speak Spanish for work reasons, or simply to add one more skill to their resumes. Without a doubt, learning to speak a language as popular as Spanish is one of the best things that we are going to be able to do for our professional careers. Since in this globalized world in which we live today we have to have all those skills that allow us to work from anywhere in the world and thus, have many more opportunities.

Of course, we are not only going to need to learn these topics if we are learning for business because if we are doing it for personal reasons we must also know all these terms and phrases so that we can communicate in a much more effective way. Business topics today are very common in everyday conversations, so it is very important that we know how to recognize each one of them so that we are not caught off guard when someone is talking to us about business in Spanish. In the same way, we are going to see some things that are related to regular labor issues, as well as various topics related to family ties, relationships, and of course, social networks, which are so popular today.

Possessive Pronouns

Possessive pronouns in Spanish work the same way as they do in English, they replace the noun of the sentence. These are the same as the tonic possessive adjectives, and they have the same meaning. However, they're used in sentences where there's no noun. We'll go over these pronouns and then we'll illustrate this with a couple of examples.

Personal	Possessive	Pronunciation	Translation
Yo	Mío	Mee-oh	Mine
Tú	Tuyo	Too-yoh	Yours
Usted	Suyo	Soo-yoh	Yours
Él/ Ella/ Eso	Suyo	Soo-yoh	His/ Hers/ Its
Nosotros	Nuestro	Nooehs-troh	Ours
Ustedes	Suyo	Soo-yoh	Yours
Ellos/ Ellas	Suyo	Soo-yoh	Theirs

El mío está guardado en mi bolso.

Ehl meeoh ehstah gooahr-dah-doh ehn mee bohl-soh.

Mine is kept in my bag.

El tuyo quedó mejor después de tu corte de cabello.

Ehl too-yoh keh-doh meh-hohr dehs-pooehs deh too cohr-teh deh cah-beh-yoh.

Yours was better after your haircut.

Nosotros veremos a los nuestros esta navidad.

Noh-soh-trohs beh-reh-mohs ah lohs nooehs-trohs ehs-tah nah-bee-dahd.

We'll see our family this Christmas.

Como pudimos ver al principio de esta sección, cuando aprendimos acerca de las formas correctas de pronunciar y escribir cada uno de esos pronombres posesivos, vemos que hay muchos que se repiten, pero que sin embargo, según el sujeto de la oración, van a tener diferentes significados. Muchas personas tienen algunos pequeños problemas con esto, por lo cual debemos estar bien atentos para evitar caer en esos pequeños errores que nos puedan llevar a traducir alguna información de forma incorrecta, o simplemente a tener algunos problemas a la hora de expresar algún mensaje.

Telling Time

Knowing how to tell the time is something much more important than is often believed. I mean, people may think that this is basic and not that important, however, in the business world, it's important to know how to make appointments and all that. In the same way, if we are going to see a friend or family member, we must tell them what time we expect them, and that way we will be much more organized. Not many things are more important in the world of business than telling the time and setting up appointments. We must learn how to tell the time in Spanish.

What Time Is It?

These are a couple of examples of how to ask for the time:

¿Qué hora es?

Keh oh-rah ehs

What time is it?

Disculpe, ¿podría por favor decirme la hora?

Dees-cool-peh poh-dree-ah pohr fah-bohr deh-seer-meh lah oh-rah

Excuse me, could you please tell me the time?

¿Qué hora marca el reloj?

Keh oh-rah mahr-cah ehl reh-loh

What time does the clock show?

Parts of a Day

It's important to learn how to tell morning, afternoon, evening, and night:

Mañana	Mah-gnaa-nna	Morning
Mediodía	Meh-deeoh-dee-ah	Noon
Tarde	Tahr-deh	Afternoon
Atardecer	Ah-tahr-deh-sehr	Sunset
Noche	Noh-cheh	Night
Medianoche	Meh-deeah-noh-cheh	Midnight
Madrugada	Mah-droo-gah-dah	Early morning
Amanecer	Ah-mah-neh-sehr	Sunrise

Telling the Time

The usual way to tell time is by dividing the twenty-four hours into two halves, AM for the morning and PM for the afternoon/ night. Time in Spanish is told by the following pattern: hours in numbers + "y" (and) + minutes in the hour.

In this respect, you can always say the number of minutes. There are also names for a specific number of minutes. In particular, when it's the hour "o'clock" this is replaced by the expression "en punto" (at that point).

Here are some examples of times and how they're told in Spanish:

07:00 AM	Siete AM en punto	See-eh-teh ah-eh-meh ehn poon-toh
08:40 PM	Ocho y cuarenta PM	Oh-choh ee cooah-rehn-tah peh-eh-meh
03:15 PM	Tres y cuarto PM	Trehs ee cooahr-toh peh-eh-meh
12:45 AM	Un cuarto para la una AM	Oon cooahr-toh pah-rah lah oo-nah ah-eh-meh
05:30 AM	Cinco y media AM	Seen-coh ee meh-deeah ah-eh-meh

We'll go over a couple of examples regarding time:

Quiero que llames al cliente a las siete de la mañana.

Kee-eh-roh keh yah-mehs ahl clee-ehn-teh ah lahs see-eh-teh deh lah mahn-neeah-nah.

117

I want you to call the client at seven AM.

La reunión será a las cuatro y media.

Lah reh-oo-neeohn seh-rah ah lahs cooah-troh ee meh-deeah.

The meeting will be at four-thirty.

Quiero el informe a las tres y cuarto.

Kee-eh-roh ehl een-fohr-meh ah lahs trehs ee cooahr-toh.

I want the paper at quarter past three.

Professions

Next, we are going to see a list that contains the majority of the professions, or at least the most popular, so that we can have a much broader idea of the professions most used in everyday conversations. Each of these professions is usually the most used since they are the most popular in most countries, although, of course, we must know that there are many other professions besides these, but that we have decided to only mention some of the most popular for don't make this section so long and tedious.

We may have already heard some of these professions mentioned in a television series, or even in a song, so we will realize that while some of these may be a bit difficult to pronounce, most are quite basic and contain few syllables. Best of all, in the examples section, we are going to see the context in which we could use each of these words. In the same way, we are going to see that there are certain professions that are pronounced the same as in English, as well as others that, although they are written exactly the same, have a slightly different pronunciation.

Profession	Pronunciation	Translation
Conductor	Cohn-dooc-tohr	Driver
Abogado	Ah-boh-gah-doh	Lawyer
Artista	Ahr-tees-tah	Artist
Contador	Cohn-tah-dohr	Accountant
Periodista	Peh-reeoh-dees-tah	Journalist
Dentista	Dehn-tees-tah	Dentist
Director	Dee-rech-tor	Director
Doctor	Dohc-tohr	Doctor
Enfermero	Ehn-fehr-meh-roh	Nurse
Cartero	Cahr-teh-roh	Mailman
Empresario	Ehm-preh-sah-reeoh	Businessman
Secretario	Seh-creh-tah-reeah	Secretary
Policía	Poh-lee-see-ah	Police officer
Mesero	Meh-seh-roh	Waiter
Mecánico	Meh-cah-nee-coh	Mechanic
Programador	Proh-grah-mah-dohr	Programmer
Ingeniero	Een-heh-nee-eh-roh	Engineer
Vendedor	Behn-deh-dohr	Salesman

Here are a couple of phrases using professions:

Tenemos una cita con el abogado a las dos de la tarde.

Teh-neh-mohs oo-nah see-tah cohn ehl ah-boh-gah-doh ah lahs dohs deh lah tahr-deh.

We have an appointment with the lawyer at two o'clock in the afternoon.

Te desempeñarás como vendedor en esta compañía.

Teh deh-sehm-pehn-neeah-rahs coh-moh behn-deh-dohr ehn ehs-tah cohm-pahn-neeah.

You'll perform as a salesman in this company.

Agenda una cita con mi secretaria.

Ah-hen-dah oo-nah see-tah cohn mee seh-creh-tah-reeah.

Set an appointment with my secretary.

Te presento a mi contadora, trabajarás con ella de ahora en adelante.

Teh preh-sehn-toh ah mee cohn-tah-doh-rah trah-bah-hah-rahs cohn eh-yah deh ah-oh-rah ehn ah-deh-lahn-teh.

I present to you my accountant, you'll work with her from now on.

Relevant Business Phrases

In this section, what we are going to see are some of the most popular phrases that we are going to use in terms of everything related to business. Of course, these phrases are going to be very necessary if we are learning to speak Spanish for work issues. However, if this is not the case, it will also be necessary for us to learn all these topics since we will be able to use them in any instance that comes our way in our work or in any other

120

circumstance of our daily lives. The good thing is that each of these phrases is easy to learn and that we will be able to use all the words that we learned earlier when we were talking about the professions.

In other words, below we are going to see the grammatical structures and sentences that we can use in each of the cases that we want to talk about the professions mentioned above. We are going to realize that, unlike previous sections, in this section, we have included many examples so that in this way we have a practical guide on each of the situations in which we can talk about professions, as well as the easier ways on how we can pronounce each of those phrases.

Soy graduado en leyes.

S-oh-ee grah-dooah-doh ehn leh-yehs.

I have a degree in law.

Le dejé el informe en el escritorio de su oficina.

Leh deh-heh ehl een-fohr-meh ehn ehl ehs-cree-toh-reeoh deh soo oh-fee-see-nah.

I left the report for him on his office desk.

Tiene mucho trabajo que hacer y está llegando tarde.

Tee-eh-neh moo-choh trah-bah-hoh keh ah-sehr ee ehs-tah yeh-gahn-doh tahr-deh.

You have a lot of work to do and you're running late.

La reunión será a las tres de la tarde.

Lah reh-oo-neeohn seh-rah ah lahs trehs deh lah tahr-deh.

The meeting will be at three PM.

Estoy desempleado, busco trabajo aquí.

Aest-oh-e daes-am-plae-do boos-coh trah-bah-hoh ah-keeh.

I'm unemployed, I'm looking for a job here.

La despidieron ayer y su amiga renunció hoy.

Lah dehs-pee-dee-eh-rohn ah-yehr ee soo ah-mee-gah reh-noon-seeoh oh-ee.

She got fired yesterday, and her friend resigned today.

Necesitamos que firme el contrato, por favor.

Neh-seh-see-tah-mohs keh feer-meh ehl cohn-trah-toh pohr fah-bohr.

We need you to sign the contract, please.

Yo dejé un currículum aquí la semana pasada.

Yoh deh-heh oon coo-rree-coo-loom ah-kee lah seh-mah-nah pah-sah-dah.

I left a resume here last week.

Que pase el siguiente candidato a la entrevista de trabajo.

Keh pah-seh ehl see-gee-ehn-teh cahn-dee-dah-toh ah lah ehn-treh-bees-tah deh trah-bah-hoh.

Let the next candidate for the job interview come in.

Buenas tardes. ¿Por qué busca trabajar en esta compañía?

Booeh-nahs tahr-dehs pohr keh boos-cah trah-bah-hahr ehn ehs-tah cohm-pahn-neeah

Good afternoon. Why are you looking to work in this company?

Está contratado, nos vemos la próxima semana.

Ehs-tah cohn-trah-tah-doh nohs beh-mohs lah proh-xee-mah seh-mah-nah.

You're hired, see you next week.

Family Tree

Without a doubt, family is one of the most important things we have in life. In any country in the world, and in whatever language we are speaking, we are going to need to know how to pronounce the different terms used for relatives, as well as knowing the proper pronunciation for each of these. One of the main differences that the familiar April has in Spanish compared to English is that cousins have different terms depending on whether they are feminine or masculine. In English, the word cousin encompasses both the feminine and the masculine, but in Spanish these are different depending on each case.

Beyond that, the truth is that there are not many differences in the grammatical structures that are found in each case, but we must be alert to learn each of these words perfectly so that we can address our relatives or the relatives of another person correctly. Without a doubt, these are words that we are going to use on a daily basis since in everyday conversations it is very common to refer to a family member or a close person. Similarly, in the examples, we are going to see some of the most repeated phrases when we talk about a family member so that we know where to insert each of these words in a conversation or in a sentence. We'll start by teaching you how to talk about your relatives.

Profession	Pronunciation	Translation
Madre	Mah-dreh	Mother
Padre	Pah-dreh	Father
Abuela	Ah-booeh-lah	Grandmother
Abuelo	Ah-booeh-loh	Grandfather
Hermana	Ehr-mah-nah	Sister
Hermano	Ehr-mah-noh	Brother
Hija	Ee-hah	Daughter
Hijo	Ee-hoh	Son
Tía	Tee-ah	Aunt
Tío	Tee-oh	Uncle
Prima	Pree-mah	Cousin (female)
Primo	Pree-moh	Cousin (male)
Sobrina	Soh-bree-nah	Niece
Sobrino	Soh-bree-noh	Nephew

Other Relatives

Relative	Pronunciation	Translation
Padrastro	Pah-drahs-troh	Father-in-law
Madrastra	Mah-drahs-trah	Mother-in-law
Esposa	Ehs-poh-sah	Wife
Esposo	Ehs-poh-soh	Husband

Hermanastra	Ehr-mah-nahs-trah	Sister-in-law
Hermanastro	Ehr-mah-nahs-troh	Brother-in-law
Yerna	Yehr-nah	Daughter-in-law
Yerno	Yehr-noh	Son-in-law
Madrina	Mah-dree-nah	Godmother
Padrino	Pah-dree-noh	Godfather

We'll go over a couple of family-related phrases:

Tus hijos están más grandes cada vez que los veo.

Toos ee-hos ehs-tahn mahs grahn-dehs cah-dah behs keh lohs beh-oh.

Your children are bigger every time I see them.

Mi abuela hornea las mejores galletas del mundo.

Mee ah-booeh-lah ohr-neh-ah lahs meh-hoh-rehs gah-yeh-tahs dehl moon-doh.

My grandmother bakes the best cookies in the world.

Sal a la sala, tu padrino te trajo un regalo.

Sahl ah lah sah-lah too pah-dree-noh teh trah-hoh oon reh-gah-loh.

Come out to the living room, your godfather brought you a present.

Mi mamá nos está invitando a todos los primos a la playa.

Mee mah-mah nohs ehs-tah een-bee-tahn-doh ah toh-dohs lohs pree-mohs ah lah plah-yah.

My mother is inviting all of us cousins to the beach.

Social Media

Without a doubt, one of the things that people use the most on a daily basis is social networks. It doesn't matter if we are in school, if we are in university, if we are parents or if we are older adults since each of us uses at least one social network daily. Of course, not all of us use the same social networks, but it is important that we know some of the terms and phrases that are related to all these topics since conversations about these topics can arise in any member and we have to be prepared. Many times people believe that social networks are just for seeing photos or news, but the truth is that they often help us connect with people from other countries and make business relationships or any other type of thing. That is why learning to pronounce all the phrases and words related to social networks is something fundamental today, especially since we live in a world that is always connected through the internet.

For example, if we go to eat at a restaurant, we are likely to ask what their Instagram account is or if they have a Facebook page. The same goes for every other tourist attraction we go to, as well as every conversation we have with our friends and family. That's why we'll study some terms relevant to social media and then we'll go over a couple of phrases that are extremely useful to use social media in Spanish.

Phrases Relevant to Social Media

No compartas tu clave con nadie.

Noh cohm-pahr-tahs too clah-beh cohn nah-dee-eh.

Don't share your password with anyone.

Yo te sigo en Instagram.

Yoh teh see-goh ehn eens-tah-grahm.

I follow you on Instagram.

Me gusta lo que publicas en Twitter.

Meh goos-tah loh keh poo-blee-cahs ehn tooee-tehr.

I like what you post on Twitter.

Comparte mi publicación de venta, por favor.

Cohm-pahr-teh mee poo-blee-cah-seeohn deh behn-tah pohr fah-bohr.

Please share my sales post.

Vamos a conectarnos en LinkedIn.

Bah-mohs ah coh-nehc-tahr-nohs ehn leen-kehd-een.

Let's connect on LinkedIn.

No publiques esa fotografía por favor.

Noh poo-blee-kehs eh-sah foh-toh-grah-fee-ah pohr fah-bohr.

Don't post that photograph, please.

Chapter Exercises

Eng/Spa Matching

Match these words in English with their equivalent terms in Spanish

#	English Term	Letter	Spanish Term
1	Accountant	A	Mediodía
2	Aunt	B	Abuela
3	Morning	C	Abogado
4	Son	D	Ingeniero
5	Lawyer	E	Publicar
6	Nurse	F	Noche
7	Noon	G	Hijo
8	Account	H	Periodista

9	Secretary	I	Perfil
10	Engineer	J	Tía
11	Journalist	K	Mañana
12	Post	L	Cuenta
13	Night	M	Contador
14	Grandmother	N	Enfermero
15	Profile	O	Secretario

Fill in the Blanks

Answer the questions by filling in the blanks.

1. The word "mío" is a ____ in the following sentence: "Tu perro y el mío juegan cada vez que se ven".
2. The word "tuya" is a ____ in the following sentence: "La casa tuya vive durmiendo en la sala de estar".
3. Tell these following times in Spanish: 08:36 AM, 04:15 PM, 09:12 AM.
4. How would you ask someone to add him on Facebook and follow him on Twitter in Spanish?

5. How would you set a meeting in your office at 05:00 PM in Spanish?

Translation

Write the Spanish translation of these English phrases.

1. My grandfather and my dad look very much alike.
2. The mechanic told us that our car would be ready next Friday.
3. I want you to introduce me to your boss on LinkedIn.
4. We'll be leaving on our fishing trip by dawn.
5. Tomorrow morning we'll have a "bring your son to the office" day.

Chapter 6 – Answer Key

The answers for the Eng/Spa Matching exercises are the only ones that are strict. The other answers usually allow some freedom to adapt and rephrase the sentences as long as the core concept is intact.

Eng/Spa Matching

1:M, 2:J, 3:K, 4:G, 5:C, 6:N, 7:A, 8:L, 9:O, 10:D, 11:H, 12:E, 13:F, 14:B, 15:I

Fill in the Blank

1. Possessive pronoun.
2. Possessive adjective.

3. Ocho y treinta y seis de la mañana, cuatro y cuarto de la tarde, y nueve y doce de la mañana.
4. ¿Podría agregarte en Facebook y seguirte en Twitter?
5. La reunión de hoy será a las cinco de la tarde en la oficina.

Translation

1. Mi abuelo y mi padre se parecen mucho.
2. El mecánico nos dijo que nuestro coche estaría listo para el próximo viernes.
3. Quiero que me presentes a tu jefe en LinkedIn.
4. Estaremos saliendo en nuestro viaje de pesca para el amanecer.
5. Mañana en la mañana tendremos un día de "trae a tu hijo a la oficina".

De igual forma, a continuación vamos a ver el ejemplo de una conversación entre dos personas que están hablando de algunos de los tópicos que aprendimos en este capítulo, como por ejemplo cuestiones relacionadas al trabajo y a las redes sociales. De esta forma vamos a poder ver cómo todas las frases y palabras aprendidas en este capítulo nos van a servir para desarrollar e interactuar en conversaciones habituales y así poder interpretar todo lo que nos dicen.

Muchas veces las personas creen que porque no están aprendiendo a hablar español por cuestiones laborales entonces no necesitan saber este tipo de cosas, pero la verdad es que siempre serán importantes ya que pueden surgir en cualquier conversación que tengamos, bien sea con un amigo, colega o algún familiar. En la conversación que vamos a ver a continuación, como de costumbre, primero la vamos a ver en español y luego en inglés, para que así sepamos de forma perfecta la traducción de cada una de las cosas que dicen, y podamos tomar nota de aquellas frases o estructuras gramaticales que nos parezcan interesantes.

Example of a Conversation Related to Businesses

Freddie: John, ¿dónde pusiste los documentos que había dejado encima del escritorio? ¡Los necesito urgentemente!

John: Hace una hora vino el jefe y me pidió que le entregara esos documentos. Me dijo que los necesitaba para poder realizar el informe acerca del nuevo cliente.

Freddie: No debió haberlos llevado, ya que aún no he terminado de redactar todo lo que hacía falta para el informe del nuevo cliente. Supongo que ahora tendré que pasarle esa información a través de un email.

John: Lamento mucho oír eso. La verdad no sabía que esos documentos estaban incompletos.

Freddie: ¿Sabes cuál es la ocupación del nuevo cliente? Necesito saber esa información para así poder saber qué incluir en el informe.

John: He oído que el nuevo cliente es un ingeniero químico que trabaja en una empresa farmacéutica. Pero la verdad es que nunca lo he conocido, así que mejor deberías preguntarle directamente al jefe para asegurarnos que de verdad es un ingeniero.

Freddie: Perfecto, voy a preguntarle al jefe para así incluir ese dato en el informe.

John: Genial. También puedes ver la información que aparece en el perfil de LinkedIn del cliente, ahí probablemente salga cuál es su trabajo.

Freddie: ¿Qué es LinkedIn?

John: Es una red social con motivos laborales en donde las personas pueden hacer networking y conocer a otras personas de la industria. Deberías abrir una cuenta.

Freddie: La verdad nunca había oído hablar de esa red social, pero suena muy interesante, voy a abrir mi cuenta ahora mismo.

John: Genial, Freddie, avísame si necesitas ayuda.

Translation

Freddie: John, where did you put the documents that I had left on the desk? I need them urgently!

John: An hour ago the boss came and asked me to give him those documents. He told me that he needed them to be able to make a report about the new client.

Freddie: He shouldn't have brought them, since I haven't finished writing everything that was needed for the new client's report yet. I guess now I'll have to pass that information on to him via email.

John: I'm so sorry to hear that. The truth is I didn't know that those documents were incomplete.

Freddie: Do you know what the new client's occupation is? I need to know that information so I can know what to include in the report.

John: I heard that the new client is a chemical engineer who works for a pharmaceutical company. But the truth is that I have never met him, so you should ask the boss directly to make sure that he really is an engineer.

Freddie: Perfect, I'm going to ask the boss to include that information in the report.

John: Great. You can also see the information that appears in the client's LinkedIn profile, it will probably show what their job is.

Freddy: What is LinkedIn?

John: It is a social network for work purposes where people can network and meet other people in the industry. You should open an account.

Freddie: The truth is that I had never heard of that social network, but it sounds very interesting, I'm going to open my account right now.

John: Great Freddie, let me know if you need any help.

CHAPTER 7:

SPORTS AND HOBBIES

Without a doubt, sports, and physical activities are some of the most important things in life. All these activities not only allow us to maintain a healthy lifestyle but also allow us to relax and enjoy our free time much more. In general, people who are fans of some sport usually practice it. That is, if someone is a big fan of basketball, it is very likely that person meets with his friends or family to play basketball from time to time. However, there are many people who like to do physical activities but are not sports fans. That is to say, there are people who usually go to the gym every day, go for a run or simply do any other physical activity, and although they like it a lot, it is very unlikely that they will ever watch a baseball game or play a game of football with their friends.

The important thing is that whatever our passion is in the world of sports or physical activities, it is very important that we learn the correct way in which we should use each term related to sports, since many times they are usually pronounced in a different way to how we would do it in English. However, this is a subject that can be learned quickly, since the words are usually not that difficult and the phrases used in this context are also usually simple.

Of course, you may not like sports or you are not a person who likes physical activities. That is totally understandable, but we must know that knowing each of these terms is extremely important since they can be present in any type of daily conversation. It may be that a friend is telling us about his passions, that we are talking to a family member, that we are watching television or something else, and it is very possible that some topic related to sports will come up. In fact, in many countries, there are sports that are part of the culture, and we must know to say that we truly visited those countries.

For example, if we go to Argentina or Brazil, soccer is part of the culture of both countries, since people do not see it as a simple game or a simple sport, but for them, it is something sacred. In fact, in Argentina they often say that soccer is a religion for them, so we can see people of all ages enjoying a game in the stadiums at any time of the day. The same happens in Brazil since soccer is one of the things that has lifted more children out of poverty and has allowed them to dream of a bright future. The point is, if we ever visit those two countries, we should know some super important terms around the world of sports.

Football: Fútbol americano

Basketball: Baloncesto

Soccer: Fútbol

Tennis: Tenis

Golf: Golf

Baseball: Béisbol

Score: Anotación

Goal: Gol

Net: Malla

Baseball bat: Bate

Ball: Pelota

Glove: Guante

Basket: Aro

Points: Puntos

Runs: Carreras

Home run: Jonrón

Field: Terreno

Stadium: Estadio

Sports: Deportes

Gym: Gimnasio

Workout: Ejercicio

Training: Entrenamiento

Athlete: Atleta

Marathon: Maratón

Running: Correr

Game: Juego

Play: Jugar

Field goal: Gol de campo

Game over: Juego terminado

Sports are a fundamental section when learning a sport, since they will always be necessary topics in any type of conversation. Similarly, not only will they be very important in regular conversations, but it is very likely that we will also hear about all these topics in movies or television series. We will have realized in this section that most sports have general terms that are said in the same way in each of the languages, and that is why they do not have a specific translation into Spanish, such as touchdown, which is a term that is always used in English.

However, the vast majority of other sports have specific terms for each of the things that we must learn to say in Spanish. Best of all is that each of these words is very easy to learn since it is very likely that we have heard or seen them before. Of course, if we are fans of sports or physical activities, it will be even easier since we may be familiar with some of these terms.

Phrases Related to Sports

As well as knowing how to pronounce and write the main sports, it is also very important that we know what are some phrases and words related to sports and physical activities. It is very likely that when we have conversations related to sports or different physical activities, some of these phrases or words will come up, which is why it is very important that we not only know how to pronounce them but also know their meaning. We may have heard these phrases a few times on television, on social networks, or even in a television series. Of course, it is very rare that we watch television or use social networks in another language, but this can help us a lot to continue developing our Spanish-speaking skills.

In the same way, many times when we watch international sports or we are watching foreign television channels, we have no choice but to interpret what they are saying based on the context of the conversion. On the other hand, if we learn all these phrases perfectly, we will be making sure that we do not have any problem related to the fluency of our understanding in each of these conversations or situations. Of course, as we have done in previous chapters, at the end of this section we are going to see some sentences and examples that will allow us to better understand all this.

Winner: ganador

Loser: perdedor

Player: jugador

Sore loser: mal perdedor

¡Gané!: I won!

Let's go!: ¡Vamos!

Rendirse: giving up

Win: ganar

Lose: perder

Effort: esfuerzo

Fun: diversión

Sweat: sudor

Algunos ejemplos que podemos dar en relación a estos tópicos son los siguientes:

Mario scored a goal last night in his soccer game.

Mario anotó un gol en su juego de fútbol anoche.

She was having a lot of fun while she was swimming in the pool.

Ella estaba divirtiéndose mucho mientras estaba nadando en la piscina.

He is a sore loser, he needs to change thy and behave better.

El es un mal perdedor, necesita cambiar y comportarse mejor.

You can see the effort she is putting in every day at the gym.

Puedes ver el esfuerzo que ella está haciendo todos los días en el gimnasio.

He sweats too much when he goes to the gym.

Él suda mucho cuando va al gimnasio.

How to Ask Someone His/Her About Favorite Sport

Believe it or not, most people love to talk about their favorite sports and physical activities they do every day. This is undoubtedly one of the most common topics in everyday conversations, as people like to talk about their favorite team, the previous day's baseball game, or the routine they did in the gym. That's why it's important to know how to ask the right questions when we want to learn more about a person's lifestyle or passions.

In fact, this is a very useful topic when we are getting to know someone since we will want to know what their main hobbies are, as well as the things that person is interested in. People love to talk about their passions, as they are things that are very important to them and that have a deep meaning in many cases. That is why if we know how to ask people questions about their favorite sports or physical activities, it not only guarantees us that we will be able to make many new friends, but we will also be able to understand and interpret much better what our friends tell us.

What's your favorite sport?: ¿Cuál es tu deporte favorito?

What's your favorite physical activity?: ¿Cuál es tu actividad física favorita?

Which days do you go training?: ¿Qué días vas a entrenar?

What's your favorite team?: ¿Cuál equipo es tu favorito?

How often do you work out?: ¿Qué tan seguido entrenas?

Sin duda alguna, cada una de esas frases y palabras se pueden utilizar en cualquiera de las conversaciones habituales que tengamos con alguien, sin importar si nos gustan los deportes o no, al igual que no importa de lo que estemos hablando ya que son temas que pueden surgir de forma espontánea. Si nos enfocamos en aprender todas estas cosas, entonces estaremos preparados para poder desarrollar e interpretar de la mejor manera cualquier conversación en donde puedan surgir algunos de estos temas, ya que como hemos dicho de forma repetida, no importa si no somos fanáticos de los deportes o no hacemos alguna actividad física, estos temas suelen ser bastante comunes en cada una de las conversaciones.

De igual forma, a continuación vamos a ver un ejemplo de una conversación en donde dos personas se encuentran hablando acerca de estos temas, para que así podamos ver un contexto de una conversación que puede surgir en cualquier momento, y podamos ver en donde introducir cada una de esas frases, palabras y oraciones. Primero, la vamos a ver en español, y luego tendremos la traducción en inglés para que podamos ver de forma práctica cómo utilizar cada una de estas frases y oraciones.

Example of a Conversation Related to Sports and Physical Activities

José: ¡Hola! ¿Cómo estás Peter? Tanto tiempo sin verte.

Peter: ¡Hola José! Estoy muy bien, gracias por preguntar. ¿Tú cómo estás?

José: Muy bien, Peter. Hace un rato estaba en el gimnasio y en unas horas voy al partido de béisbol con mi hermano.

Peter: ¡Qué bueno, José! ¿Te gustan otras actividades físicas o sólo el gimnasio?

José: A veces voy a correr por el parque, a hacer CrossFit o alguna de esas actividades que exigen un poco más de esfuerzo, pero por lo general sólo voy al gimnasio.

Peter: ¡Me parece excelente! Yo solía ir al gimnasio hace algunos años, pero desde que nació mi hijo menor no he ido más. Tengo que intentar volver algún día de estos, la verdad me gustaba mucho ir al gimnasio.

José: De verdad es algo muy bueno. En el gimnasio no sólo te diviertes y entrenas, sino que también liberas mucho estrés de tu cuerpo.

Peter: Eso es correcto José. ¿Vas al partido de béisbol de los Tigres?

José: ¡Sí! ¿Tú también vas?

Peter: No, lo voy a ver por televisión ya que no logré conseguir entradas.

José: Bueno está bien. ¡Espero que ganen los Tigres!

Peter: ¡Yo también!

Translation

Jose: Hi! How are you Peter? Long time no see.

Peter: Hi Jose! I'm very good, thanks for asking. How are you?

Jose: Very good Peter. A while ago I was in the gym, and in a few hours I'm going to the baseball game with my brother.

Peter: Good job Jose! Do you like other physical activities or just the gym?

José: Sometimes I go for a run in the park, do CrossFit or one of those activities that require a little more effort, but usually I just go to the gym.

Peter: Sounds great to me! I used to go to the gym a few years ago, but since my youngest son was born I haven't been there anymore. I have to try to go back one of these days, I really liked going to the gym.

José: It really is a very good thing. In the gym you not only have fun and train, but also release a lot of stress from your body.

Peter: That's right Jose. Are you going to the Tigers baseball game?

Jose: Yes! Are you going too?

Peter: No, I'm going to watch it on TV since I couldn't get tickets.

Jose: Well that's fine. I hope the Tigers win!

Peter: Me too!

CONCLUSION

Without a doubt, learning a new language is one of the most wonderful things we can do, especially when it comes to a language as popular as Spanish. Of course, English is the most widely spoken language in the world, but Spanish is one of the main ones and one of the languages that has become more relevant in recent times. As we all know, the world has gone through a process of globalization in recent years, which is why today it is much easier to be in contact with other cultures, languages, people, and much more around the world.

That is why learning a new language will not only help us expand our knowledge and entertain ourselves, but it will also help us open up new job opportunities since the language will not be a limiting barrier for us. Of course, it's also fine that we want to learn this language just out of curiosity or because we just like to know about other cultures. The most important thing of all is that learning a new language is useful for many things, and there is no age limit in which we must learn it since we can do this whenever we want.

After having read this book, we are undoubtedly in a position to say that we can speak Spanish perfectly, as long as we never forget that we must constantly practice so that we do not forget everything we have learned. The problem of many of the people who start learning new languages is that they believe that it is

144

only enough to read a book like this, attend a course or something similar to speak another language perfectly when the truth is that practice is what will lead us to perfection.

Knowing how to speak a language, but not practicing it, is like having muscles and not exercising them, because sooner or later if we don't go to the gym or do some physical activity then we will lose those muscles. The good news is that, as we have said several times throughout the book, each of us can practice consistently and easily through many different methods.

In the same way, it is very important to emphasize that learning a new language is not only good from a professional point of view and that it will be very useful in other facets of our lives, but it is also something that will help us strengthen our mind in many ways. For example, it is proven that when we learn a new language, our memory is strengthened, since we have to learn many completely new words, grammatical structures, sentences, and phrases. Similarly, when we learn a language we also increase our ability to do different tasks at the same time and increase our level of proactivity. As we all know, learning a new language requires a lot of attention and effort, just like learning to think in another language. That is why when we are learning Spanish we are also going to strengthen our ability to do several things at the same time.

Finally, it is also important that we know that many times learning a new language will help us a lot to improve our performance in other types of academic activities since it increases our level of concentration and the mental effort we make to learn. The point of all this is that we must know that learning a language not only helps us in terms of professional and personal growth but also helps us a lot in terms of our mental health.

Without a doubt, this path may not be easy at first, since learning a new language also requires a lot of patience and discipline, because otherwise, we will not be able to achieve our goals. But if we have enough discipline to practice every day, as well as the necessary level of patience to not give up in the middle of the process, without a doubt we will be able to achieve all those results that we want to achieve, and we can become bilingual. What do you say? Are you ready to start on this wonderful adventure? If your answer was yes (and I'm sure it was) then I'm sure you will achieve every one of your goals.

BONUS CHAPTER
(ARTICLES)

In this chapter, the objective is that we see some articles that we can use to practice our reading in Spanish, as well as different aspects of our pronunciation. In the same way, this is an excellent technique that will help us a lot to not only exercise our reading level and our pronunciation, but we will also be able to learn many new words and phrases that are commonly used in Spanish. Without a doubt, this is one of the most effective techniques that we can use when we are learning a new language, and that is why we have decided to include it in this book.

The important thing, so that we can get the most out of this section, is that we can try to understand and interpret each of the sentences that appear in the text that is in Spanish, and so that later we can verify if we understood everything perfectly when we are reading the English translation. Many people underestimate the power of reading, but it can help us achieve great things, especially when it comes to reading in another language since in this way we will understand everything we have been learning throughout this book. in a better way. On the other hand, if we do not focus on understanding each of these things, it is very likely that we will forget many of the phrases and words that we have learned so far.

La Evolución de la Música Latina (The Evolution of the Latin Music)

Sin duda, la historia de la música latina es muy extensa y muy interesante. A diferencia de muchísimos otros géneros musicales, la música latina es una de las más movidas y emocionantes del mundo artístico. De hecho, muchas personas alrededor del mundo se fascinan cuando escuchan este tipo de música, ya que sienten una vibra positiva en el cuerpo que se genera gracias a los variados ritmos latinos que se producen en estos géneros musicales. Entre los más famosos de la música latina tenemos a la salsa, la bachata, el reggaetón, el tango, la cumbia y muchos otros que han sido los géneros encargados de representar no sólo a la música sino a la cultura latina alrededor del mundo.

Sin embargo, muchos de esos géneros son más famosos en algunos países y menos escuchados en otros. Por ejemplo, el tango es uno de los géneros musicales más famosos de Argentina, pero la verdad es que es muy poco escuchado en otros países. En cambio, la bachata es uno de los géneros musicales más escuchados en República Dominicana y en otros países del Caribe. Es por eso que cada país tiene una música en específico que se encarga de representar a la cultura y de expresar lo que la gente piensa y siente.

Sin duda alguna, la música tiene el poder de transportarnos a otros lugares y de hacernos sentir muchísimas emociones que no se pueden sentir con ningún otro tipo de arte. Lo qué pasa con la música latina es que está llena de alegría y de muchos colores, que nos generan una enorme satisfacción al escucharla. Es por eso que la música latina se ha ido expandiendo hacia muchos otros países en el mundo, y ha sido bien recibida por el público internacional. Hoy en día hay artistas que son escuchados en todo el mundo, como por ejemplo, Bad Bunny, Ozuna, J Balvin, Maluma, Daddy Yankee y otros más que representan al género musical del reggaetón.

Por supuesto, existen muchos otros géneros que se han ido popularizando alrededor del mundo, pero el reggaetón tiene la principal característica de que es un estilo de música que es muy popular entre los jóvenes, cuyos artistas se han vuelto muy famosos en las principales plataformas digitales como por ejemplo Spotify, Apple Music, Deezer y muchos otros. Sin duda alguna, es probable que hayamos escuchado alguna de esas canciones en la radio, en la televisión o en esas principales plataformas digitales. Popularmente se dice que nunca es un mal día para escuchar música latina, así que debemos seguir ese consejo para alegrar cada uno de nuestros días.

Translation

Without a doubt, the history of Latin music is very extensive and very interesting. Unlike so many other musical genres, Latin music is one of the busiest and most exciting in the art world. In fact, many people around the world are fascinated when they listen to this type of music, since they feel a positive vibe in the whole body that is generated thanks to the varied Latin rhythms that are produced in these musical genres. Among the most famous musical genres of Latin music, we have salsa, bachata, reggaeton, tango, cumbia and many others that have been the genres in charge of representing not only music but also Latin culture around the world. world.

However, many of those genres are more famous in some countries and less listened to in others. For example, tango is one of the most famous musical genres in Argentina, but the truth is that it is rarely heard in other countries. Instead, bachata is one of the most listened to musical genres in the Dominican Republic and in some Caribbean countries. That is why each country has a specific music that is responsible for representing the culture and expressing what people think and feel.

Without a doubt, music has the power to transport us to other places and make us feel many emotions that cannot be felt with any other type of art. What happens with Latin music is that it is full of joy and many colors, which give us enormous satisfaction when listening to it. That is why Latin music has been expanding to many other countries in the world, and has been well received by the international public. Today there are artists who are heard all over the world such as Bad Bunny, Ozuna, J Balvin, Maluma, Daddy Yankee and others who represent the musical genre of reggaeton.

Of course, there are many other genres that have become popular around the world, but reggaeton has the main characteristic that it is a style of music that is very popular among young people, whose artists have become very famous on the main digital platforms. such as Spotify, Apple Music, Deezer and many others. Without a doubt, it is likely that we have heard some of those songs on the radio, on television or on those main digital platforms. It is popularly said that it is never a bad day to listen to Latin music, so we must follow that advice to brighten each of our days.

La Historia de las Capitales Sudamericanas (The History of the South American Capitals)

Sin duda alguna, Sudamérica es uno de los continentes más interesantes del mundo, ya que cuenta con países increíbles, culturas interesantes, y sobre todo, gente que es muy cálida y que tienen un carisma increíble. Sin embargo, lo verdaderamente impresionante de este continente son todas las capitales hermosas que tiene a lo largo de todos sus territorios y países. Debemos recordar que Sudamérica está compuesto por 10 países principales y, adicionalmente, otros países no tan conocidos como Surinam y Guyana. Una de las capitales más importantes (y más famosas) del continente es Brasilia. La mayoría de las personas usualmente cree que la capital de Brasil es Rio de Janeiro, pero la verdad es que la ciudad de Brasilia es una de las más hermosas del continente, pese a no compararse con el paraíso tropical de Río de Janeiro.

Luego, una de las capitales más bonitas no sólo de este continente sino del mundo entero es Buenos Aires. Esta es una ciudad cargada de bastante historia y cultura en la que podemos ver muchísimos recitales de tango, comer una de las mejores carnes del mundo, y por supuesto, ver un partido de fútbol en vivo y sentir la enorme pasión de los fanáticos argentinos. Todo esto hace que Buenos Aires sea uno de los destinos preferidos por muchos viajeros del continente, por lo que es muy recomendable que cuando podamos, no dudemos en visitar esta hermosa ciudad.

Luego tenemos a Bogotá, que es la capital de Colombia. Esta es una ciudad que se caracteriza por tener uno de los mejores cafés del mundo, así que si algún día vamos, no podemos dejar de probar el exquisito café de la marca Juan Valdez, que es uno de los cafés más aclamados en el mundo entero. De igual forma, el clima de Bogotá hará que simplemente queramos vivir ahí por siempre. Unos kilómetros más al sur, nos vamos a encontrar con Montevideo, que es la capital de Uruguay. En los últimos años, esta es una ciudad que ha tenido un crecimiento económico impresionante, lo que ha llevado a muchísimas personas del continente a emigrar a ese país en búsqueda de mejores oportunidades laborales y de aumentar el nivel de sus estilos de vida. De igual forma, esta es una ciudad que tiene muchísimos destinos turísticos por recorrer, por lo cual es un destino sumamente recomendado para todo tipo de personas.

Por último, tenemos a Quito, que es la capital de Ecuador. Esta es una ciudad bastante famosa alrededor del mundo, ya que hay un punto en el que existe lo que se le conoce como la mitad del mundo. Es decir, cuando visitemos ese parque, nos vamos a dar cuenta que hay una enorme línea amarilla, que indica que en ese mismo punto estamos parados en la mitad del mundo. De igual forma, Ecuador tiene muchísimos sitios turísticos que vale la pena recorrer, tales como Machu Pichu y muchas otras obras arquitectónicas ancestrales que hacen que este país sea único y maravilloso. Estas fueron tan solo cinco de las capitales más importantes e históricas de Sudamérica, que no debemos dudar en visitar si alguna vez se nos presenta la oportunidad.

Translation

Without a doubt, South America is one of the most interesting continents in the world, as it has incredible countries, interesting cultures, and above all, people who are very warm and have incredible charisma. However, what is truly impressive about this continent are all the beautiful capitals that it has throughout all its territories and countries. We must remember that South America is made up of 10 main countries, and additionally other less well-known countries such as Suriname and Guyana. One of the most important (and most famous) capitals of the continent is Brasilia. Most people usually believe that the capital of Brazil is Rio de Janeiro, but the truth is that the city of Brasilia is one of the most beautiful on the continent, despite not being compared to the tropical paradise of Rio de Janeiro.

Then, one of the most beautiful capitals not only in this continent but in the whole world is Buenos Aires. This is a city full of history and culture, where we can see many tango recitals, eat one of the best meats in the world, and of course, watch a live soccer game and feel the enormous passion of Argentine fans. All this makes Buenos Aires one of the favorite destinations for many travelers from the continent, so it is highly recommended that when we can, we do not hesitate to visit this beautiful city.

Then we have Bogotá, which is the capital of Colombia. This is a city that is characterized by having one of the best coffees in the world, so if one day we go, we cannot miss out on trying the exquisite coffee from the Juan Valdez brand, which is one of the most acclaimed coffees in the entire world. Similarly, the climate of Bogotá will make us simply want to live there forever. A few kilometers further south, we will find Montevideo, which is the capital of Uruguay. In recent years, this is a city that has had impressive economic growth, which has led many people from the continent to emigrate to that country in search of better job opportunities and to increase the level of their lifestyles. Similarly, this is a city that has many tourist destinations to visit, which is why it is a highly recommended destination for all types of people.

Finally, we have Quito, which is the capital of Ecuador. This is quite a famous city around the world, as there is a point where there is what is known as the middle of the world. That is to say, when we visit that park, we are going to realize that there is a huge yellow line, which indicates that at that same point we are standing in the middle of the world. Similarly, Ecuador has many tourist sites that are worth visiting, such as Machu Picchu and many other ancient architectural works that make this country unique and wonderful. These were just five of the most important and historical capitals of South America, which we should not hesitate to visit if the opportunity ever arises.

La Mejor Comida Hispana (The Best Hispanic Food)

Una de las mejores cosas que tienen los países hispanohablantes es, sin duda alguna, la comida. La gran mayoría de los países latinoamericanos, al igual que países de Centroamérica, México y España se caracterizan por tener una gastronomía privilegiada, cuyos amantes van mucho más allá de sus fronteras. Cuando hablamos de la buena comida hispana, no nos referimos a esas falsas imitaciones que podemos encontrar en Taco Bell, Chipotle, La Cantina o alguno de estos restaurantes o franquicias. En cambio, nos estamos refiriendo a la verdadera comida hispana, hecha por las personas que de verdad saben darle una buena sazón a esa comida, y usan los típicos ingredientes de cada uno de esos países.

Por supuesto, puede que aún no hayamos probado algunos de esos platos, pero en este artículo vamos a hacer un repaso por algunos de los mejores platos hispanos. Uno de esos es la empanada argentina. Este es un plato bastante típico que consiste en un pastel de masa que está relleno de diversos ingredientes previamente cocinados y que sirve caliente. Esto se puede comer como entrada, aperitivo o simplemente una comida fuerte si nos comemos varias empanadas. Estas no sólo son famosas en Argentina, sino que también las podemos encontrar en otros países como Colombia y Venezuela.

Otra de las mejores comidas hispanas es el Ceviche peruano. Esto consiste en un tipo de pescado picado en trocitos, acompañado de otros ingredientes como limón, papas, arroz y muchas otras cosas. Sin duda alguna, muy pocas recetas de pescado son tan deliciosas como el ceviche peruano, ya que simplemente es algo único. Otro plato típico es el de la Bandeja Paisa en Colombia, que es un plato que incluye huevo, salchicha, arroz, aguacate y muchas otras cosas deliciosas que nos van a dejar muy satisfechos.

Por último, tenemos a los tamales, que son una de las comidas mexicanas más deliciosas. Estos están hechos a base de harina de maíz y suelen estar rellenos con carne o pollo, al igual que diversas salsas a base de aguacate e ingredientes variados. Sin duda alguna, no podemos dejar de comer alguno de esos deliciosos platos si tenemos alguna vez la oportunidad, ya que sencillamente no nos vamos a arrepentir. De igual forma, podemos buscar todas esas recetas en YouTube e intentar hacerlas en casa, ya que sin duda alguna también será un experimento que valga la pena.

Translation

One of the best things that Spanish-speaking countries have is, without a doubt, the food. The vast majority of Latin American countries, as well as countries in Central America, Mexico and Spain are characterized by having a privileged gastronomy, whose lovers go far beyond their borders. When we talk about good Hispanic food, we are not referring to those false imitations that we can find in Taco Bell, Chipotle, La Cantina or any of these restaurants or franchises. Instead, we are referring to real Hispanic food, made by people who really know how to give that food a good seasoning, and use the typical ingredients of each of those countries.

Of course, we may not have tried some of those dishes yet, but in this article we are going to take a look at some of the best Hispanic dishes. One of those is the Argentine empanada. This is a fairly typical dish that consists of a dough cake that is filled with various previously cooked ingredients, and served hot. This can be eaten as a starter, an appetizer or simply a strong meal if we eat several empanadas. These are not only famous in Argentina, but we can also find them in other countries such as Colombia and Venezuela.

Another of the best Hispanic foods is the Peruvian Ceviche. This consists of a type of fish chopped into small pieces, accompanied by other ingredients such as lemon, potatoes, rice and many other things. Without a doubt, very few fish recipes are as delicious as Peruvian ceviche, as it is simply something unique. Another typical dish is the Paisa Tray in Colombia, which is a dish that includes eggs, sausage, rice, avocado, and many other delicious things that will leave us very satisfied.

Finally, we have tamales, which are one of the most delicious Mexican foods. These are made from corn flour, and are usually filled with meat or chicken, as well as various avocado-based sauces, and assorted ingredients. Without a doubt, we cannot stop eating any of these delicious dishes if we ever have the opportunity, since we simply will not regret it. In the same way, we can look for all those recipes on YouTube and try to make them at home, since without a doubt it will also be a worthwhile experiment.

El Fútbol, Deporte Rey en Argentina (Soccer, the King of Sports in Argentina)

Sin duda alguna, el fútbol es el deporte más popular en Argentina y es el encargado de hacer vibrar a la sociedad en cada uno de los partidos que disputan los equipos más populares del país. Pese a que Argentina solo ha ganado dos copas mundiales en la historia, es uno de los países que tiene futbolistas más talentosos alrededor del mundo, teniendo entre los más famosos a dos de los mejores jugadores de la historia como Diego Maradona y Lionel Messi. Estos dos jugadores, uno que lastimosamente falleció en 2020 y el otro que aún sigue activo, han llevado no solo la pasión del deporte argentino alrededor del mundo, sino que también se han encargado de esparcir un poco de cultura de ese país hacia otros rincones del mundo, incluyendo a países de Europa, Asia y África.

De hecho, el estadio de Nápoles, que es uno de los estadios de fútbol más importantes en Argentina, se llama Estadio Diego Armando Maradona en honor a este enorme jugador que es considerado el mejor jugador en la historia de ese equipo. Por otro lado, Lionel Messi es considerado el mejor futbolista en la actualidad y de la historia por muchos expertos en ese deporte.

En Argentina, se dice usualmente que el fútbol no es solo un deporte, sino que es como una religión para todos los argentinos. No importa qué edad tengas, cuál es tu religión, tu nivel de educación o tu nivel económico, si eres argentino es muy probable que te guste el fútbol. De hecho, tan solo en la Ciudad de Buenos Aires (que es la capital de Argentina) hay más de 50 equipos de fútbol profesionales. Esto nos habla de la enorme pasión que genera este deporte, al igual que la enorme cantidad de dinero que se mueve en torno a este maravilloso deporte. De hecho, los canales de televisión en Argentina básicamente sólo hablan de fútbol, ya que saben que es el deporte que más le interesa a las personas.

Los dos equipos argentinos más famosos son Boca Juniors y River Plate (ambos de la Ciudad de Buenos Aires). Ambos son considerados como los equipos más importantes de la historia en el fútbol sudamericano, ya que las personas saben que estos no solo han sido los equipos con más trofeos en la historia del continente, sino que también son los equipos con más aficionados no solo en Argentina sino en Sudamérica. Los argentinos dicen que no podemos ir al país y no ir a un partido de fútbol, ya que sería similar a ir a París y no ver la Torre Eiffel. El punto es que si vamos a Argentina, no podemos dejar de ir a un emocionante partido de fútbol, ya que sin duda alguna estaremos conociendo uno de los aspectos más importantes de la cultura argentina.

Translation

Without a doubt, soccer is the most popular sport in Argentina, and it is responsible for making society vibrate in each of the matches played by the most popular teams in the country. Despite the fact that Argentina has only won two world cups in history, it is one of the countries that have the most talented soccer players around the world, having among the most famous two of the best players in history such as Diego Maradona and Lionel Messi. These two players, one who unfortunately passed away in 2020 and the other who is still active, have not only brought the passion of Argentine sports around the world, but have also been responsible for spreading a bit of culture from that country to other corners of the world. world, including countries in Europe, Asia and Africa.

In fact, the stadium in Naples, which is one of the most important soccer stadiums in Argentina, is called Estadio Diego Armando Maradona, in honor of this huge player who is considered the best player in the history of that team. On the other hand, Lionel Messi is considered the best footballer today, and also the best in history by many experts in the sport.

In Argentina, it is usually said that soccer is not just a sport, but rather it is like a religion for all Argentines. No matter how old you are, what your religion is, your level of education or your economic level, if you are Argentine it is very likely that you like soccer. In fact, in the City of Buenos Aires alone (which is the capital of Argentina), there are more than 50 professional soccer teams. This tells us about the enormous passion that this sport generates, as well as the enormous amount of money that moves around this wonderful sport. In fact, the television channels in

Argentina basically only talk about soccer, since they know that it is the sport that most interests people.

The two most famous Argentine teams are Boca Juniors and River Plate (both from the City of Buenos Aires). Both are considered as the most important teams in the history of South American football, as people know that these have not only been the teams with the most trophies in the history of the continent, but they are also the teams with the most fans not only in Argentina but in South America. Argentines say that we cannot go to the country and not go to a football match, since it would be similar to going to Paris and not seeing the Eiffel Tower. The point is that if we go to Argentina, we can't stop going to an exciting soccer game, since without a doubt we will be getting to know one of the most important aspects of Argentine culture.

Complete Spanish Phrasebook
+ Digital Spanish Flashcards Download

Scan QR code above to claim your free bonuses

—————— OR ——————

visit exploretowin.com/vipbonus

Ready To Start Speaking Spanish?

**Inside this Complete Spanish Phrasebook
+ digital Spanish flashcards combo you'll:**

✓ **Say what you want:** learn the most common words and phrases used in Spanish, so you can express yourself clearly, the first time!

✓ **Avoid awkward fumbling:** explore core Spanish grammar principles to avoid situations where you're left blank, not knowing what to say.

✓ **Improved recall:** Confidently express yourself in Spanish by learning high-frequency verbs & conjugations - taught through fun flashcards!

Scan QR code above to claim your free bonuses

—————— OR ——————

visit exploretowin.com/vipbonus

REFERENCES

Alger, N. (2017, May 2). 7 Best Ways To Learn Spanish (Like a Pro). Spanishland School. https://spanishlandschool.com/best-ways-to-learn-spanish/

Kostiuk, K. (2019, April 28). The Fastest, Most Direct Way to Learn a New Language in 8 Lightning-quick Steps. FluentU Language Learning. https://www.fluentu.com/blog/fastest-way-to-learn-a-new-language/

Learning Spanish? Here are 6 tips to help you. (2017, March 16). Bilingua. https://bilingua.io/tips-learning-spanish

Sherman, M. (2014, October 30). Learning a language – 10 things you need to know. The Guardian. https://www.theguardian.com/education/2014/oct/30/learning-another-language-ten-tips

Top 10 Tips for Learning Spanish. (n.d.). StudySpanish.com. https://studyspanish.com/topten_tips

Made in United States
North Haven, CT
08 September 2022

23905241R00105